# AMERICAN BUREAUCRACY

# American Bureaucracy

*By*

# PETER WOLL

BRANDEIS UNIVERSITY

NEW YORK

W · W · NORTON & COMPANY · INC ·

TO
*Robert and Lucinda*

# Contents

# Preface

THIS BOOK examines one of the most important developments in modern American government, the growth of the national bureaucracy to a dominant position in areas that traditionally have been thought properly reserved to Congress, the President, and the Judiciary. American bureaucracy is deeply involved in the political process, a fact all too often overlooked or underplayed in the literature of political science. The political activities of administrative agencies are of overwhelming significance today and present problems in constitutional and political theory of current importance.

Virtually every aspect of our daily lives is regulated to some degree by one or the other of the numerous administrative agencies that make up the national bureaucracy. The powers of these agencies are extensive, being judicial and legislative in nature as well as executive. The Constitution states that these fundamental powers of government should be separated into three branches that have effective checks and balances in relation to each other. Otherwise, arbitrary government will prevail. The growth of a bureaucracy outside of the original constitutional scheme throws this neat and logical system out of kilter. It has become essential to understand the role of bureaucracy in our government in order to appreciate the meaning of fundamental changes that have taken place in the American system of constitutional democracy.

Hopefully, this book will be of interest to all—students, scholars, and the general reader—who are concerned with the increasing political involvement of the bureaucracy in our government. It may be used effectively as supplementary reading in all college courses where the examination of this problem is considered relevant. In American government courses, it provides material that contrasts with that of the traditional textbook. It may also be used in such courses as part of a series of books that deal with particular aspects of American government. In public administration courses, it may be used as a core book where the case method is employed or as supplementary reading to contrast with a basic text.

I am in debt to many for the interest I have in studying bureaucracy, and some have been particularly instrumental in molding my emphasis upon the political role of the administrative branch. My initial excitement about this area came from Herman M. (Red) Somers at Haverford College, who combined insight and personal experience to make the study of public administration come alive. Arch Dotson guided my intellectual inquiries into this subject with great perception and understanding. And Clinton Rossiter has deepened my appreciation of the American constitutional and political tradition, which is so important to a proper grasp of the present role of the bureaucracy. This book was read in manuscript by Richard H. Leach, who made many valuable suggestions that helped immeasurably in preparing the final draft. It is hardly necessary to add that all facts and interpretations presented are my responsibility.

Peter Woll

Pacific Palisades, California

# AMERICAN BUREAUCRACY

# CHAPTER 1    The Nature of Bureaucracy and Constitutional Government

THE OFTEN quoted passage from Alexander Pope's *Essay on Man* states:

> For forms of government let fools contest;
> What'er is best administer'd is best.

Following this eighteenth century expression of opinion, the nineteenth century classical economists, in their zeal for a governmental system based upon the principle of *laissez faire,* might well have said:

> For forms of government let fools contest;
> What'er is *least* administer'd is best.

Although today many Americans, perhaps with the amusingly expressed ideas of C. Northcote Parkinson ("Parkinson's Law") in mind, tend to agree with the latter rather than the former, developments since Pope's day make his couplet more meaningful than may appear at first glance. In modern industrialized societies, regardless of the particular forms of government in operation the *bureaucracy* [1] or the administrative arm of the government seems to be assuming more and more power at the expense of the legislative and judicial branches. Further, the increasing power of bureaucracy has reduced in many instances the influence of the main executive bodies of these societies. Bureaucracy can not be dismissed as simply part of the "executive branch" of government controlled by the President or the Cabinet. [2]

1. The term "bureaucracy" will be used throughout this book to designate "governmental bureaucracy," unless otherwise specified.
2. For a discussion of the role of bureaucracy in Russia, France, and Great Britain, see Eric Strauss, *The Ruling Servants* (New York: Frederick A. Praeger, 1961).

In the United States the growth of a vast administrative branch has introduced an important new political force into the governmental system, a force which might well become dominant if it is not controlled. This chapter will consider the political nature of administrative functions with reference to American bureaucracy and then the relationship between the functions of the administrative branch and the American constitutional system.

## Administrative Functions: The Political Nature of Bureaucracy

In all nations with developed bureaucracies, "administrators" are deeply involved in politics—in the attempt to solidify and expand their power within other branches of the government and over the general public. Politics concerns itself with the nature, sources, use, and distribution of power. Power has been aptly defined as "participation in the making of decisions." [3] Decisions, in turn, involve the effective *implementation* as well as determination of policy, since a non-implemented decision is not very meaningful.

The political nature of bureaucracy is initially revealed in the behavior of administrative agencies acting as interest groups, and in individual behavior within administrative agencies. Administrative agencies come into contact with various external groups, both governmental and nongovernmental. To retain their power, or to expand, all agencies must maintain a balance of political support over opposition. [4] Congress controls finances and has ultimate power over reorganization; thus the agencies always seek political support that can be exerted on Congress. They are responsive to the President, or his coordinating staff agencies such as the Bureau of the Budget, only insofar as they are essential to the maintenance of political support. Agencies that have strong interest group support outside the bureaucracy do not generally have to rely on the President or his staff agencies. On the other hand, some agencies without adequate outside group

3. Harold D. Lasswell and Abraham Kaplan, *Power and Society* (New Haven: Yale University Press, 1950).

4. For an excellent case study illustrating this point see Samuel P. Huntington, "The Marasmus of the ICC," 61 *Yale Law Journal* 467–509 (1952).

support must substitute presidential support in order to survive. One important determinant of presidential control over any particular administrative agency is the extent of the agency's contact with and support from private interest groups.[5] The effectiveness of this control, of course, will vary with the power of the private groups concerned and their ability to influence Congress or the courts.

The activity of individuals within organizations also reveals the political nature of bureaucracy. Though these individuals are assigned formal roles, such roles are frequently and easily short-circuited by those attempting to maintain, solidify, or expand their positions, in the same way that the organization as a whole plays a political game to advance its own interests.[6]

Another aspect of the political nature of bureaucracy lies in the fact that the functions these agencies perform involve a direct exercise of legislative, judicial, and executive power, all of which have profound consequences to the community as a whole. The bureaucracy is not merely carrying out law; rather it is deeply involved in the determination, interpretation, and execution of law.

## THE LEGISLATIVE FUNCTIONS OF
## ADMINISTRATIVE AGENCIES

The legislative function involves the formulation of general rules applicable to the community as a whole. This function may be distinguished, as will be noted below, from the more specific nature of the judicial function. The exercise of the legislative function affects the community on a compulsory basis, for the state is a compulsory association; thus legislation or law-making involves significant governmental power over the citizenry.

The Constitution, in Article I, gives the law-making power initially to Congress; however, Congress was never supposed to have a monopoly of it. The President, through the veto and because of his responsibility to recommend legislation to Congress,

5. For an illustration of this point see "The Kings River Project," in Harold Stein (ed.), *Public Administration and Policy Development* (New York: Harcourt, Brace and Co., 1952), pp. 533–572.

6. For further information see Victor A. Thompson, *Modern Organization* (New York: Alfred A. Knopf, 1961), chaps. vii–viii.

*Saves Congress for Political death.*

was given highly significant law-making power in Article II. Further, the framers of the Constitution recognized the implications of judicial interpretation of congressional acts, which formally became part of the constitutional system in 1803 through Marshall's broad definition of the nature and scope of judicial review in *Marbury v. Madison*.[7] The major point of the constitutional separation of powers was that while Congress would have the primary responsibility toward legislation, both the President and the Supreme Court had a measure of control in the law-making process. Congress therefore could not become an arbitrary legislative body.

Although Congress possesses the primary legislative power, it can delegate its power to the executive or administrative branch. Any such delegation of power must be made within certain limits, and must provide standards of conduct so specific that the agency concerned, and if necessary the courts upon judicial review, can ascertain the intent and scope of the congressional grant of authority. In this way, theoretically, Congress still retains the primary legislative power, and is merely appointing an agent to act for it; in fact, however, virtually complete legislative discretion is given to the designated agency or to the President.

Almost any agency exercising regulatory functions can be used to illustrate how legislative power resides in administrative hands. When obvious need for regulation arises, and when pressure from a variety of groups is exerted on Congress to act, it establishes an administrative agency charged with the responsibility of regulation in the area in question.

The Interstate Commerce Commission (ICC), for example, was established in 1887 to regulate the railroads because of pressure from agricultural interests that were being subjected to various types of economic coercion by the railroads. Congress was aware of the charges made against the railroads, but could not take the time to investigate them and develop minute regulations to control economic abuses; the subject was too vast, complex, and fraught with political danger. Congress decided to yield to pressures for regulation by creating an independent regulatory agency; at the same time this device prevented Congress from having to make difficult decisions involving regulation which

7. 1 Cranch 137 (1803).

would undoubtedly cause dissatisfaction in many of the groups being regulated. In the statutes creating the ICC and more recent agencies, such as the Securities and Exchange Commission, the National Labor Relations Board, and the Federal Communications Commission, Congress specified that the respective activities should be regulated in a "just" and "reasonable" manner, and in the "public interest." Thus, in allocating radio and television channels the Federal Communications Commission must heed the "public interest, convenience, and necessity." The ICC must establish rail, trucking, and shipping rates that are "just" and "reasonable." The Civil Aeronautics Board must also uphold the "public interest" in the establishment of "just" and "reasonable" air fares.

The result of this vague phraseology, which is considered sufficient in the writing of such statutes, is that the administrative agencies are permitted wide latitude in establishing regulations that are in effect legislative. This places the burden of reconciling group conflict upon the bureaucracy rather than Congress.[8] Who is to say what constitutes the "public interest," or what is "just" and "reasonable?" Congress may on occasion investigate such policy-formulation by administrative agencies; however, it is usually done sporadically, if at all. Moreover, the courts are very reluctant to interfere in what they consider to be the "policy-making" area of administrative decision making. It is hard to estimate in an exact way the significance of administrative legislation through rule making; however, the volume of such administrative legislation during any given period almost certainly equals the volume of congressional law making. The significance of such administrative legislation also may often exceed that of Congress.

The legislative function is also exercised through direct administrative involvement in initiating and drafting laws in Congress. The President's Committee on Administrative Management estimated in 1937 that at least two-thirds of all public bills passed by Congress emanated directly from the administrative branch.[9]

8. See E. Pendleton Herring, *Public Administration and the Public Interest* (New York: McGraw-Hill, 1936), pp. 6–9.

9. President's Committee on Administrative Management, *Report with Special Studies* (Washington, 1937), p. 361.

Various observers since that period have indicated that the bulk of public legislation passed by Congress does not originate there, but rather in the particular administrative agency or agencies concerned with the legislation.[10] Congressmen wishing to gain support for legislation must find allies, and the most natural place to turn to initially is the particular administrative agency or agencies that will have jurisdiction over implementation of the legislative proposals. It is not only desirable, but generally necessary, for example, to gain the support of the Veterans Administration for proposals modifying veterans' benefits; or of the Department of Agriculture for proposals concerning modification or elimination of price supports in particular areas; or of the Securities and Exchange Commission for plans to modify existing securities laws. The reasons for gaining such support are fairly complex, and center upon the close connection that exists between agencies and the groups they regulate; this frequently means there is a similarity between the interests of private groups and administrative agencies in particular areas. The congressman who gains the support of the administrative agency concerned with particular legislation thereby frequently is assured of private support. In addition to administrative facility derived as a result of specialized attention to narrow policy fields, the above practice places weapons in the hands of administrators that frequently cannot be overcome by Congress in its attempt to maintain independent judgment in law making.

The combination of direct administrative participation in the congressional process, and the willingness of Congress to delegate substantial legislative power to administrative agencies, results in the firm and significant position of governmental bureaucracy in the legislative process.

### THE JUDICIAL ROLE OF GOVERNMENTAL BUREAUCRACY

The existence, nature, and location of judicial power within a governmental system has always been an important consideration of political theory. The exercise of judicial functions, whether

10. For a balanced point of view see Ernest S. Griffith, *Congress—Its Contemporary Role* (New York: New York University Press, 1961).

by relatively independent bodies such as courts or by administrative agencies that are more directly involved in the exercise of policy and prosecuting functions, is always "political" and a vital part of any political system. The performance of the judicial function involves the use of significant governmental power.

Generally speaking, the judicial function pertains to the disposition of a *specific* case on the basis of *general* rules; thus, when the internal revenue agent settles a tax case with an individual he is specifically applying the Internal Revenue Code, a general body of rules and regulations. His act is adjudicative in nature; the Code is legislation. When the Federal Communications Commission grants a broadcast license it is exercising a judicial function, for it is deciding a relatively specific case involving a limited number of named parties on the basis of its own regulations plus such requirements as Congress may have written into the law. In a real sense a controversy is involved in the exercise of the judicial function, requiring legal disposition; without a controversy there would be no case, and hence no need for adjudication. Such a controversy does not have to be *adversary,* in the sense of placing the parties concerned into formal opposition with each other. It can be reflected in an asserted claim of an individual against the government, for example, for veterans' benefits, or disability benefits under the Social Security laws. In such a non-adversary type of case the governmental agency concerned still has to decide whether or not benefits are to be given, and if so, in what amount. On the other hand, one private party may be in controversy with another, or a government agency may feel that there is some question concerning compliance with the law on the part of an individual or group. In this case the agency will bring action against the party in question, and adjudicate the dispute between itself and the party on the basis of public policy considerations and evidence given or available to the agency.

What agencies exercise judicial functions, and what is the legal source of this form of administrative power? In general terms, judicial power is exercised on the basis of a congressional grant of authority. This is also true, as was previously noted, with regard to administrative exercise of legislative functions. Examples of important administrative exercise of judicial functions may be seen in such agencies as the Federal Trade Commission, the Interstate Commerce Commission, the Securities and Exchange Commission, the National Labor Relations Board, the Federal Communications Commission, and others usually classified as "independent regulatory commissions." In addition to these independent regulatory commissions judicial functions are exercised by numerous other agencies both independent and within the executive branch, such as the Veterans Administration, an agency which decides several million cases a year involving benefit questions. Some of these questions are routine, but in many instances administrative discretion determines the nature, amount, and recipient of particular benefits. Within the executive branch, departments such as Agriculture, Defense, and Health-Education-Welfare possess important adjudicative powers.

Through such specific application of general rules the impact of national regulation is brought home to many individuals. When significant economic interests are involved in regulation final policy is frequently implemented only through adjudication, for the stakes are high and private parties are unwilling to let governmental policy or economic competitors stand unchallenged. In terms of the day-to-day activities of the citizenry administrative adjudication is probably more ubiquitous than that carried out by courts of law, with the exception of criminal actions. Thus the prices of many services (telephone, electric, and gas utility), some food prices (milk), transportation facilities and rates, communications facilities (radio, television), banking and insurance rates and protection, are determined initially through adjudication, based on more general policy considerations. Just as Congress is unable to define standards of administrative action so precisely that administrative discretion is eliminated, the agencies themselves are unable in their regulations to be precise enough to prevent the delegation of significant discretion to adjudicative officers; thus, the process of adjudication may (and possibly should) shape policy as it is applied in individual cases. Because agencies engaged in adjudication are primarily policy-oriented, it is inevitable that an intimate relationship has grown between these two functions in the administrative process.

## THE EXECUTIVE FUNCTION AND
## GOVERNMENTAL BUREAUCRACY

Executive functions pertain to administrative activities aimed at increasing the efficiency of government in budgeting and disbursement, planning, personnel, and so on. Many agencies are solely "executive" in this sense; however, all agencies engaged in legislation and adjudication also perform executive functions, pertaining mainly to management. These functions have a profound, though often indirect, effect upon the community. Clearly nothing is more important to government than the type of personnel employed; individuals formulate legislative proposals and perform judicial functions. Planning, which is executive in character, may lead directly to administrative legislation. The budgeting process always becomes deeply involved in program planning, which in turn directly affects the legislative and judicial activities of agencies. The line may frequently be very fine between an executive and a legislative function; however, distinctions can and should be made.

Important examples of the exercise of executive functions may be found in such agencies as the State Department, all the major executive departments under the President, the Civil Service Commission, the Bureau of the Budget and the other components of the Executive Office of the President, and in such independent government corporations as the Tennessee Valley Authority (TVA). These agencies formulate over-all executive budgets, engage in long-range planning, and in general manage huge governmental enterprises. Agencies such as the Civil Service Commission generally implement congressional policy concerning personnel, and some discretion may be employed in establishing personnel regulations. Such policy may be classified as management policy, and although it affects the community as a whole in the sense of determining who may join the federal civil service and under what conditions, it is not generally discussed under the heading of administrative legislation. Similarly, TVA, an independent government corporation, implements its own plans and in this sense it "legislates"; however, once again, this form of legislation may be distinguished from more general regulatory legislation and classified as management policy. In some areas, of course, TVA engages in limited regulatory legislation, for example, when it establishes electricity rates for the region under its jurisdiction. Although in areas such as these functional distinctions become blurred, it is possible to distinguish between the "policy" formulated by administrative agencies which governs various aspects of internal management and procedure, or which is related to providing profitable operation of a government enterprise (such as TVA), and administrative legislation, which regulates on a national scale the various industries of the country.

In addition to managerial functions executive power includes the power of enforcement. The best recent illustration of this is found in the action taken by President Kennedy in the fall of 1962, when he sent troops to Oxford, Mississippi, and federalized the national guard there in order to enforce a Federal court order, directed at university authorities and state officials, to proceed with integration at the University of Mississippi. The courts have the power to declare the law, and issue court orders for relief from illegal action; however, they do not have the force necessary to carry out their orders in the face of direct defiance. The ability to employ force is a monopoly of the President and the administrative arm of the government.

## Constitutional Limitation and Bureaucratic Power

Before considering the development, structure, and operation of the administrative process at greater length, it is important to point out profound initial implications of the wide scope of administrative power on the concept of the separation of powers.

Although technical constitutional norms prevail, the constitutional system to limit governmental power through the separation of powers no longer functions in the manner or to the degree thought necessary by the framers of the Constitution. The validity of this conclusion is of central concern, for if the constitutional system functions effectively then limitation of governmental power is automatic; if, on the other hand, the original system has been altered through the expansion of bureaucratic functions, then, new devices of control of administrative power must be recognized or developed in order to maintain the constitutional ideal of limited government.

## GENERAL LEGAL IMPLICATIONS

In *The Federalist* (1787, 1788) Madison, Hamilton, and Jay were particularly concerned with the concept of the separation of powers, which they hoped would be established through the ratification of the Constitution. The separation of powers was to be the principal method of limiting the role of the national government in the republic. Madison noted in *Federalist 47* that "the accumulation of all powers, legislative, executive, and judiciary, in the same hands, whether of one, a few, or many, and whether hereditary, self-appointed, or elective, may justly be pronounced the very definition of tyranny." The Constitution, on the other hand, does not completely separate the powers of the three branches of government, but rather blends them so that each branch will be able to check the other branches by interfering with their functions. For example, the President can exercise the legislative veto; but at the same time Congress has various weapons it can use to interfere with presidential power including the right to approve of various appointments and control treaties. The judiciary's power to review both congressional and executive actions is checked by the President's power to appoint justices to the Court, the power of Congress to approve of such appointments, and finally congressional control over the structure and jurisdiction of the judiciary, including the determination of the number of justices on the Supreme Court and its appellate jurisdiction.

There is no constitutional objection to legislative power residing outside of Congress, nor is there to judicial functions being employed by extra-judicial departments. As Madison pointed out in *Federalist 47*, only "where the *whole* power of one department is exercised by the same hands which possess the *whole* power of another department, [are] the fundamental principles of a free constitution . . . subverted." The very fact that administrative agencies today are permitted to perform all the functions of government indicates that the courts have seen no constitutional objection to such a combination of legislative, judicial, and executive power in the hands of one branch, provided basic controls exist through congressional and judicial surveillance.

## BUREAUCRACY AND THE CONSTITUTIONAL SYSTEM

The implications of present-day bureaucratic power to traditional constitutional government must be viewed not only in terms of its effect upon the separation of powers mechanism, but also in relation to the theoretical basis and the broad purposes of the constitutional system. It is interesting to observe the type of situation the framers of the Constitution thought would lead inevitably to the exercise of arbitrary power. In *Federalist 47*, Madison, in supporting the idea that powers should be blended among the various branches, uses the argument that Montesquieu, who originated the separation of powers doctrine, based his system upon the British constitution of his day, which permitted a certain sharing of functions. Madison notes that the principles of a free constitution would have been subverted in the British constitution "if the king, who is the sole executive magistrate, had possessed also the complete legislative power, or the supreme administration of justice." This was not the case, however, because "the magistrate, in whom the whole executive power resides, cannot of himself make a law, though he can put a negative on every law; nor administer justice in person, though he has the appointment of those who do administer it." He adds that he agrees with Montesquieu's statement that: "Were the power of judging joined with the legislative, the life and liberty of the subject would be exposed to arbitrary control, for *the judge* would then be *the legislator*. Were it joined to the executive power, *the judge* might behave with all the violence of *an oppressor*." (Italics are Madison's.) The framers of the Constitution were willing to permit one branch to exercise a portion of the powers of a coordinate branch, provided that one of two conditions prevailed: the exercise of power constitutes a necessary check upon the coordinate branch; the power is properly incidental to the main function of the branch—for example, the judicial power of subpoena may be exercised by the legislature if it is necessary for effective law-making.

Today, instead of this rather delicate balance between the major governmental branches, there has been a major delegation of legislative and judicial power to the administrative branch by Congress for political and regulatory reasons that do not fit the traditional constitutional pattern. The power is not employed solely for the purposes of checking coordinate congressional and judicial branches, nor is it exercised merely because it is "incidental" to the "executive" function. In other words, present administrative powers do not conform to either the theory or mechanism of the separation of powers in the Constitution. The extent of this variation from the constitutional norm will be fully explored in succeeding chapters dealing with the relationships between the administrative branch on the one hand, and Congress, the judiciary, and the President on the other.

Does the statement that the constitutional system has been altered in substance and theory as a result of bureaucratic functions clash with the fact that administrative power has expanded and found no constitutional impediment? Many changes have taken place in our political system that have altered substantially traditional constitutional theory and practice. The development of political parties and interest groups and their present role in government was clearly not foreseen and is beyond the expectations and intentions of the framers of the Constitution. Also, various changes in the electoral system providing, for example, for the popular election of the President and members of the Senate are out of line with the original system. Although some of these changes, such as the direct election of senators, have resulted from constitutional amendment, most have occurred as a result of custom and usage.

There is nothing "unconstitutional" about the present characteristics of bureaucracy; but the constitutional changes which have occurred must be recognized and dealt with in terms of the broad purposes of constitutional government. The primary purpose of a constitutional system is to limit the powers of government; thus, if the original system does not function in limiting bureaucratic power, it is important to determine what, if anything, has replaced it.

## THE PREMISE OF LEGISLATIVE SUPREMACY

Two remaining aspects of the relationship between the original constitutional system and present day bureaucratic power remain to be discussed. First, it is important to note that the Constitution was framed in an atmosphere of distrust of legislative bodies and the powers they possessed. The framers of the Constitution, of course, had to work within the boundaries of political tradition; hence, the powers they assigned to Congress were necessarily based upon the powers traditionally given to legislative bodies, particularly in the colonies. Needless to say, one of the principal reasons the Constitution was ratified was the fact that it varied only slightly from many of the colonial constitutions, and incorporated a separation of powers doctrine accepted by the colonies in their own constitutions. The problem of curbing the legislature could not be approached from the standpoint of what powers should be withdrawn from it, but rather from the approach of checking inherent legislative power. The framers knew they had to give Congress certain powers and were worried about the nature and extent of these powers.

The feelings of the framers concerning the legislature are illustrated by Madison in *Federalist 48:*

> . . . In a democracy, where a multitude of people exercise in person the legislative function, and are continually exposed, by their incapacity for regular deliberation and concerted measures, to the ambitious intrigues of their executive magistrates, tyranny may well be apprehended on some favorable emergency, to start up in the same quarter. But in a representative republic, where the executive magistracy is carefully limited, both in the extent and the duration of its power; and where the legislative power is exercised by an assembly, which is inspired by a supposed influence over the people, with an intrepid confidence in its own strength; which is sufficiently numerous to feel all the passions which actuate a multitude; yet not so numerous as to be incapable of pursuing the objects of its passions, by means which reason prescribes; it is against the enterprising ambition of this department, that the people ought to indulge all their jealousy and exhaust all their precautions.
>
> The legislative department derives a superiority in our governments from other circumstances. Its constitutional powers being at

once more extensive, and less susceptible of precise limits, it can, with the greater facility, mask, under complicated and indirect measures, the encroachments which it makes on the co-ordinate departments. It is not infrequently a question of real nicety in legislative bodies, whether the operation of a particular measure will, or will not extend beyond the legislative sphere. On the other side, the executive power being restrained within a narrower compass, and being more simple in its nature; and the judiciary being described by landmarks, still less uncertain, projects of usurpation by either of these departments would immediately betray and defeat themselves. Nor is this all: as the legislative department alone has access to the pockets of the people, and has in some constitutions full discretion, and in all a prevailing influence over the pecuniary rewards of those who fill the other departments; a dependence is thus created in the latter, which gives still greater facility to encroachments of the former.

Several ideas in Madison's paper should be emphasized. First, Madison distinguishes between a democracy and a representative republic (constitutional democracy) and notes that in the former the absence of checks and balances in the system opens a path for executive domination of the legislature; hence, power seized by the executive during a time of emergency may replace the democratic process. In a constitutional democracy, on the other hand, the powers of the executive are carefully defined and limited by the constitution; thus executive usurpation is not likely to occur. The legislative branch, however, is disproportionately powerful because its democratic base provides it potentially with strong political support, which, in all probability, it will seek to use on various occasions, and its constitutional powers are necessarily vague and not capable of precise definition.

With this concept and fear of legislative power in mind the framers set about constructing a system which gave primary attention to requirements of congressional limitation. The powers of Congress were defined as carefully as possible, and although these enumerated powers later were relied upon for a vast expansion of national power their original purpose was to set the boundaries of congressional action. Moreover, Congress was established as a bicameral body, in which the interests of the House of Representatives were pitted against those of the Senate. Different powers were given to each house of the legislature, and in a sense a checks and balances system internal to Congress itself was created. Specific prohibitions were placed on congressional action, and when the Bill of Rights was added to the Constitution the first amendment set the tone:

*Congress* shall make no law respecting the establishment of religion, or prohibiting the free exercise thereof; or abridging the freedom of speech, or of the press; or the right of the people peaceably to assemble, and to petition the government for a redress of grievances. (Italics added.)

In contrast to this rather exalted view of the legislature, Alexander Hamilton noted in *Federalist 72* that although

"the administration of government, in its largest sense, comprehends all the operations of the body politic, whether legislative, executive, or judiciary, [administration] in its most usual, and perhaps in its most precise signification, . . . is limited to executive details, and falls peculiarly within the province of the executive department. The actual conduct of foreign negotiations, the preparatory plans of finance, the application and disbursement of the public monies, in conformity to the general appropriations of the legislature, the arrangement of the army and navy, the direction of the operations of war; these, and other matters of a like nature, constitute what seems to be most properly understood by the administration of government."

Keeping in mind this limited view of executive power, and concentration upon the importance of the legislature, the *premises* of the constitutional system are no longer valid today. This is a further reason to support the view that present bureaucratic power does not fit neatly into the pattern of limited government established by the Constitution of 1789.

## THE ROLE OF MOTIVATION IN THE CONSTITUTIONAL SYSTEM

The framers of the Constitution realized that it would not be enough simply to enable each branch of government to check coordinate branches in order to maintain the separation of powers; the branches must be motivated to remain independent and oppose any move on the part of other branches directed at limiting their sphere of power. It was assumed that institutions, as well as individuals, act in accordance with what they conceive to be their own self-interest; therefore, the framers attempted to shape what would be the political self-interest of each branch in such a way that it would jealously guard its prerogatives against encroachment. As Madison noted in *Federalist 51* the aim of the separation of powers system is "to divide and arrange the several offices in such a manner, as that each may be a check on the other; that the *private* interest of every individual, may be a sentinel over the *public* rights." (Italics added.) *Federalist 51* expands this concept in the following way:

But the great security against a gradual concentration of the several powers in the same department, consists in giving those who administer each department, the necessary constitutional means, and personal motives, to resist encroachments of the others. The provision for defence must in this, as in all other cases, be made commensurate to the danger of attack. Ambition must be made to counteract ambition. The interest of the man must be connected with the constitutional rights of the place. It may be a reflection on human nature, that such devices should be necessary to control the abuses of government. But what is government itself, but the greatest of all reflections on human nature? If men were angels, no government would be necessary. If angels were to govern men, neither external nor internal controls on government would be necessary. In framing a government, which is to be administered by men over men, the great difficulty lies in this: You must first enable the government to control the governed; and in the next place, oblige it to control itself.

Conflicting interests, based upon different electoral constituencies, powers, and terms of office, were theoretically to motivate branches to maintain independent status.

How does this constitutional system of motivation compare with the operation of the governmental branches today? It is true that there is a great deal of conflict between the President and Congress as a direct result of the constitutional separation of powers; however, this system of motivated conflicts tends to break down in the interaction of the bureaucracy and Congress. Many agencies are creatures of Congress and relatively independent of both presidential and judicial control; in these cases Congress and its particular committees involved feel no compelling need to oppose bureaucratic interests, but rather there is a definite tendency to establish a mutually satisfactory *modus vivendi*. The fact that Congress has delegated a substantial amount of its power to the bureaucracy by itself reflects both the necessities of modern democracy and the lack of fear of bureaucracy in Congress. Admittedly, there exists a common and generally unchallenged assumption that the typical congressman is highly suspicious of the "bureaucrat"; in practice however, most congressmen recognize the necessity of working with the administrative branch, and some attempt to extend their own political power, particularly with constituents, through the bureaucracy. Insofar as government action may be taken in any policy field, and with respect to any private interest or in any area of the country, it must finally stem from the administrative branch; thus, it is natural for congressmen and others to attempt to influence administrative agencies, as a means of securing implementation of policy in their interests.

For these reasons the picture of present relationships between Congress and the administrative branch is often one not of conflict based upon different personal political interests, but one of cooperation for the purposes of securing mutual political objectives. This is not to suggest that there is anything "wrong" or even "unconstitutional" about such legislative-bureaucratic cooperation. Moreover, the goals that both congressional and administrative politicians seek are not always "personal," or oriented directly to securing group advantages, but frequently are what these individuals feel is in the "national interest." Often national and group interests coincide in the minds of politicians. These considerations do not change the fact that the original system of motivation to maintain the separation of powers does not function today in the area of legislative-bureaucratic relationships.

Finally, although it is not explicitly stated in the Constitution, some of the framers felt that judicial review should play an important role in the limitation of government. Judicial review extends to certain decisions of the executive and administrative arms of the government, as well as to congressional acts. It can take place only where there is a "case and controversy." Theoretically, the courts are to judge the constitutionality and legality of challenged administrative decisions that can reasonably be presumed to fall within judicial competence; thus, they are supposed to review *legal* rather than *policy* issues. But the judiciary has found it necessary to delve into both areas, since they are frequently indistinguishable even to the most subtle minds. The courts can always find legal justification for reviewing almost any administrative decision, whether of an executive, legislative, or judicial nature; however, with the development of administrative law the possibility of judicial review and remedy of administrative action has been fundamentally altered. The courts themselves refuse to review most administrative decisions, simply because they do not have the time to consider the vast volume of cases that arise in the normal course of regulatory administration.

The expansion of administrative discretion in cases involving judicial matters has resulted from the agencies' specialization, and their ability to maintain some continuity of public policy. Despite their theoretical control, the courts are unable to limit the power of administrative agencies through the device of judicial review to the extent that many consider desirable in our constitutional system.

## The Administrative State and Constitutional Democracy

Constitutional government in the United States subsumes the democratic process; however, constitutional limitation of power concerns far more than limitation of democracy. Originally, a clear distinction was made in constitutional theory between the "democratic" component of government, which was to be the House of Representatives, and other units, which were to represent other elements of government. The states were represented by the Senate and took part in the selection of the President through the electoral college; and the judiciary was not to have a representative function at all, but in fact was to be a definite independent force to check the whims of the coordinate branches of government. Thus the Constitution was actually concerned with limiting *governments* (both national and state) as well as with limiting the direct power of the *people*.

The framers of the Constitution were aware that representatives would in many instances act independently of their immediate constituencies. Government was not conceived to be passive, even when the interests of the people were expressed directly through the elective process. But members of the House were supposed to give due consideration to their constituents in those matters where local interests were properly involved. In areas where the framers did not feel local interests relevant, or where such interests were considered detrimental to policy formulation in the national interest—as in the field of foreign affairs—they removed primary jurisdiction from the House. In matters of national significance, requiring calm deliberation, adequate information, and detachment from the influence of the people, the Senate was to fill the obvious deficiencies of the House. (See *Federalist 63*.) With respect to the legislative branch, then, democracy was to function directly only in shaping policy where the direct and immediate interests of constituents were involved. In matters of national concern requiring information in depth, and where some continuity of policy was necessary, the Senate was to exercise the leading role; it, presumably, could pay greater heed to such national concerns because of its relative isolation from the passions of the people, and because its greater tenure gave it more time to acquire necessary information and follow up initial policy decisions. By limiting the House of Representatives in this manner the ability of the *people* to participate directly in government was curbed. This limitation of democracy was intentional.

Although the direct influence of the people was to be curbed by the Senate, it should not be forgotten that Madison noted in *Federalist 51* that "a dependence on the people is, no doubt, the primary control on the government; but experience has taught mankind the necessity of auxiliary precautions." He indicates that the electoral sanction was considered to be of central importance in the control of government. In this respect the development of a bureaucracy that is not elected and that exercises broad political functions has apparently resulted in the breakdown of a primary constitutional check on arbitrary governmental power.

### THE PROBLEM OF FACTION

James Madison, in *Federalist 10*, relates the problem of constitutional democracy, that is, limited democracy, to the role of faction in society and government. He defined faction as "a number of citizens, whether amounting to a majority or minority of the whole, who are united and actuated by some common impulse of passion, or of interest, adverse to the rights of other citizens, or to the permanent and aggregate interests of the community." Faction, so defined, exists at both community and governmental levels. It becomes a serious problem, according to Madison, only when one faction becomes or threatens to become a majority:

if a faction consists of less than a majority, relief is supplied by the republican principle, which enables the majority to defeat its sinister views by regular vote. It may clog the administration, it may convulse the society; but it will be unable to execute and mask its violence under the forms of the Constitution. When a majority is included in a faction, the form of popular government, on the other hand, enables it to sacrifice to its ruling passion or interest both the public good and the rights of other citizens.

It is necessary to construct the government in such a way that a majority, once formed, will be unable to gain control of the instruments of government. For this reason a "republic" is to be favored over a "democracy."

In *Federalist 10* Madison defines a pure democracy as "a society consisting of a small number of citizens, who assemble and administer the government in person." In such a governmental system the majority, if united, can rule without limitation; hence the evils of faction will be completely uncontrolled. On the other hand a "republic," defined as "a government in which the scheme of representation takes place," may provide a cure for faction when combined with such constitutional limitations as the separation of powers and federalism. Republican government purposely checks the rule of the majority *of the people* at the same time that it prevents a combination of arbitrary governmental power. Madison notes, however, that one of the best methods of preventing arbitrary governmental power is to *limit and refine the voice of the people.* The problem of controlling faction becomes essentially one of limiting the democratic will of the community.

Madison states the crux of this matter in the following way, in *Federalist 10:*

The two great points of difference between a democracy and a republic are: first, the delegation of the government, in the latter, to a small number of citizens elected by the rest; secondly, the greater number of citizens, and greater sphere of country, over which the latter may be extended.

The effect of the first difference is, on the one hand, to refine and enlarge the public views, by passing them through the medium of a chosen body of citizens, whose wisdom may best discern the true interest of their country, and whose patriotism and love of justice will be least likely to sacrifice it to temporary or partial considerations. Under such a regulation, it may well happen that the public voice, pronounced by the representatives of the people, will be more consonant to the public good than if pronounced by the people themselves, convened for the purpose. On the other hand, the effect may be inverted. Men of factious tempers, of local prejudices, or of sinister designs, may, by intrigue, by corruption, or by other means, first obtain the suffrages, and then betray the interests, of the people.

Madison goes on to point out that in a large republic factions will be increased, but also dispersed, which will make it more difficult for any one to gain a majority in its favor. The latter consideration, concerning the problem of how to handle the *leaders,* he dismisses in *Federalist 10* with the statement that in a large republic, because it has a greater number of "fit characters," more representatives will be "fit" than "unfit." Also leaders were to be controlled through the separation of powers system.

Perhaps the most important implication of bureaucratic power and organization today is that in relation to constitutional theory and methods pertaining to the control of faction. Because of Madison's negative definition of faction, which included both political parties and interest groups, it was assumed that faction would operate to the detriment of the community as a whole. To an extent there was a feeling that any group looking after its own interests would automatically be operating against the "public interest." Federalism was to control faction through dispersion of interests geographically; and the separation of powers was to prevent any unified group from gaining control of the national governmental apparatus.

One of the central problems of dealing with this concept today is that present definitions of "faction" differ, at least in terms of emphasis, from that contained in *Federalist 10;* and, more significantly, present attitudes regarding the desirability of "faction" are totally different from Madison's original viewpoint. Generally, a political interest group today is defined as any group with shared attitudes advocating particular political goals, and methods for achieving political ends.[11] It should be realized that there are both public and private interest groups, and that any discussion of the problems of reconciling political interest groups must deal, for example, as much with the Department of Defense (or its subdivisions) as with General Dynamics Corporation; as much with the Department of Agriculture and its subdivisions as with the Farm Bureau Federation; as much with the Federal Communications Commission as with the American Telephone and Telegraph Company, the National Broadcasting Company, and the numerous other private groups within the jurisdiction of the FCC. Of course there are various differences between the public and private sectors; however, both conform to the generally accepted definition of political interest groups given above. One of the most complex and important implications of the rise of the administrative branch is the proliferation of such public interest groups.

## THE BUREAUCRACY AND CONSTITUTIONAL DEMOCRACY

The initial constitutional problem that has been raised concerning bureaucratic power is its tendency to tip the balance between coordinate branches of *government*. It was noted that the administrative branch adds a fourth dimension to the constitutional system of separation of powers, a dimension which is not controlled within its framework. Because separation of powers was intended as a curb on democratic majorities, the question of democratic control is deeply involved in the enlargement of the administrative arm of government. For example, if it could be shown that the democratic "will of the people" controls administrative decision making, the scope of the democratic process would be far greater in the present system, and the limits far less, than those established in the Constitution.

Before considering the relationship between the bureaucracy and the democratic process it is important to point out that one of the major features of constitutional development has been the

11. David B. Truman, *The Governmental Process* (New York: Alfred A. Knopf, 1953), p. 33.

expansion of the democratic base of the major institutions of government at both the national and state levels. This expansion has fundamentally altered original constitutional intent; thus, when considering the office of the President today perhaps the most significant implication of presidential power is the fact that it stems from the broadest base of democratic support in the world. If one were to analyze presidential power in relation to constitutional norms it would be necessary to point out that the original system of limitation of democracy was based upon the premise that the House of Representatives alone would be subject to direct democratic influence; hence, the House was carefully controlled by the Constitution. But once democratic influence shifts from the House to coordinate branches, the President and the Senate, the nature of constitutional limitation changes. A system designed to limit democratic majorities in the House may no longer be effective in limiting democratic power expressed through the President. It is necessary to define in outline the present position of the bureaucracy in relation to constitutional democracy in a similar manner, in order to complete a framework for the more detailed analysis that will follow.

First, the original plan of the framers of the Constitution, which limited direct democratic influence to matters of local concern, is no longer accepted. The democratic election of the Senate and the President attests to this, as does the development of political parties. It is generally agreed that "the people" should participate indirectly in public policy formulation through the selection of political leaders. In this respect constitutional democracy today emphasizes the more positive aspects of popular participation rather than requirements of limitation of the people's will. This fact, however, only appears to make it more difficult to reconcile the position of the bureaucracy with the needs of constitutional democracy, for the administrative arm of government is deeply involved in the formulation of public policy and is not in many instances controlled in any meaningful way by the elected organs of government. To the extent that these two conditions prevail it is necessary either to determine alternative methods of democratic participation, or to bring bureaucracy more under the control of the elected branches of government, if a system of constitutional democracy is to remain in existence. Before reaching this stage of value judgment, however, it will be necessary to indicate in detail the role of bureaucracy in policy formulation and the relative powers to control the bureaucracy residing in the executive and legislative branches, the only ones elected by the people. These discussions of "what is" must preface any consideration of "what ought to be." The needs of bureaucracy must be balanced with the requirements of democracy.

Insofar as the control of faction is concerned, it is widely recognized that public and private interest groups *work together* in many policy fields to achieve common goals. Because of requirements of specialization the interest groups concerned with particular policy fields are frequently unconcerned with policy formulation in neighboring areas. It is quite possible, for example, that policy formulated by the Interstate Commerce Commission pertaining to railroads, trucking, or shipping will not interest those concerned with communications policy under the jurisdiction of the Federal Communications Commission; thus, the interests which determine ICC policy will be relatively free to do as they choose. This, obviously, is not always the case; however, it occurs with sufficient frequency that it may be stated as a meaningful generalization. The development of bureaucracy, then, has greatly increased "faction," or interest groups, and at the same time it has strengthened the power of such groups in their particular policy areas.

What does the Constitution have to say about this situation? Its provisions pertaining to the control of faction do not regulate this type of administrative action. In fact, paradoxically, the Constitution encourages interest group activity beyond the sphere of its own influence. The constitutional system discourages the development of any unified source of political power in the form of disciplined political parties, or "majorities" as the framers would have said, with the ability to control the *entire governmental system*. This enables portions of that system to be governed by "factions" or political interest groups. Federalism and the separation of powers have prevented the creation of disciplined *national* parties by giving primary strength to state political organizations, and by preventing any kind of effective cohesion at the national level. The latter situation is the direct result of such constitutional provisions as different electoral constituencies for the House, Senate, and the President; staggered terms of office; and the assignment of different powers to the various branches of government. These same provisions, however, do nothing to prevent political interest groups, private and public, from operating with relative freedom at the national level. What the framers clearly failed to predict was the demise of local interest groups and the development of groups with a national orientation. The advantage of a republic because of the geographical dispersion of interests is no longer valid in the limitation of "faction."

Finally, the separation of powers system, by placing Congress in the position of an adversary of the President, motivates the legislature to place a significant portion of the administrative branch outside of the legal sphere of presidential control. In this manner, the separation of powers idea, instead of limiting governmental power, results in the relative independence of the administrative branch by displacing the most natural focal point of control. Because of the attachment between private clientele groups and public bureaucratic interest groups, the constitutional separation of powers often leads directly to an increase of "faction" in government. This situation is a further reflection of the fragmentation of power in the constitutional system, and its inability to identify a central source of political power.

## CHAPTER 2

The Development and
Organization of Bureaucracy

## The Rise of the Administrative
## Process

ALTHOUGH BUREAUCRACY has always been present in America, only
since the latter part of the nineteenth century has it assumed
characteristics recognized today as typical. There have always
been a number of executive departments exercising important
responsibilities in various areas. The War (Army), Navy, State,
and Treasury departments were created by Congress in the
eighteenth century, along with the office of Attorney General (the
Department of Justice was not established until 1870). The first
national administration under Washington included Thomas Jefferson as Secretary of State, Alexander Hamilton as Secretary of
the Treasury, Henry Knox as Secretary of War, and Edmund
Randolph as Attorney General. The activities of the departments
headed by these men generally conformed to the definition that
Hamilton gave of "administration" in *Federalist 72*, a passive concept that regarded the executive branch as an agent of Congress,
capable only of carrying out "executive details." Hamilton himself
was a vigorous and intelligent Secretary of the Treasury who
seized legislative leadership in many instances from Congress;
however, such executive initiative was due to the personality of
one man and several key followers, not to any political power
inherent in the Department of the Treasury *per se*. There is little
doubt that Hamilton believed in strong executive leadership;
while Secretary of the Treasury he was accused by Madison of
attempting to establish in the Presidency royal prerogatives equivalent to those of the King of England. Hamilton's relationship
with Congress was scored by Jefferson who, at one point, remarked
that "the whole action of the Legislature was now under the

direction of the Treasury." [1]

What in the early years of the republic depended upon the political skill of individuals in more recent times has become the responsibility of department and agency heads and their staffs automatically as a result of factors external to individual political astuteness. Thus the departments and agencies have become powerful in their own right, and although skillful political leadership may increase this power the lack of such leadership does not significantly alter their position of dominance in many areas over Congress, the President and the courts.

After the creation of the initial core of executive departments it was not until the middle of the nineteenth century that more were added. The only new department established before the Civil War was Interior, created in 1849.[2] Only at the close of the nineteenth century did a dramatic spurt begin to take place in the American bureaucratic system. Many of the most important agencies today were not created until the New Deal, and a few not until after the Second World War. Further, the deep involvement of the administrative branch in legislative and judicial functions did not take place to any significant degree until the early part of the twentieth century. Administrators, particularly department heads with political talent, exercised sporadic influence on Congress; but there was no intentional and continuous ad-

1. For the attitudes of Madison and Jefferson on Hamilton see Edward S. Corwin, *The President: Office and Powers* (4th ed., New York: New York University Press, 1957), pp. 15–18 and p. 318, n. 37.

2. The other departments were established in the following order: Justice (1870); Post Office (1872); Agriculture (1889, originally established in 1862 under the direction of a Commissioner of Agriculture); Commerce (1913); Labor (1913); Defense (1947); Health, Education, and Welfare (1953). The independent regulatory agencies date from even later in the nineteenth century: Interstate Commerce Commission (1887); Federal Reserve Board (1913); Federal Trade Commission (1914); Federal Power Commission (initially established in 1920, and made an independent agency in 1930); Federal Communications Commission (1934); Securities and Exchange Commission (1934); National Labor Relations Board (1935); Civil Aeronautics Board (1940, when it assumed part of the functions of the Civil Aeronautics Authority, created in 1938); Atomic Energy Commission (1946); Federal Aviation Agency (1958, to supersede the Civil Aeronautics Administration which was created in 1940 after the abolition of the Civil Aeronautics Authority). Note should also be made of the establishment in 1958 of the National Aeronautics and Space Administration, an independent agency that does not fall into the regulatory category.

ministrative activity in legislation and adjudication. In attempting to ascertain the reasons for the rise of the administrative process it is necessary to focus, first, upon the broad historical, economic, and political factors that have made necessary a vast expansion of bureaucracy.

## ECONOMIC DEVELOPMENT

There is a direct relationship between the nature of economic development in the United States and the rise of the administrative branch. During the first half of the nineteenth century it was possible, in general, for individual entrepreneurs to pursue goals which they considered to be in their own best interest without seriously affecting the nation as a whole. The ideal of *laissez faire* was never completely accepted, but early nineteenth century America provides one of the best historical examples of an era in which this ideal was approximated. Of course numerous private economic groups and individuals appealed directly to the government from time to time for intervention in aid of their interests, and the intermittent controversies that flared over protectionism versus free trade illustrate that even in this relatively uncomplicated economic atmosphere government was not overlooked as a potential benefactor and regulator.

After 1850 inventions and technological advances provided a catalyst for revolutionary changes, which resulted in an important alteration in the relationship between government and the economy. New industries, affecting the entire nation, in some cases required government aid and protection to become established and to prosper. The nation needed a transportation system that would span the continent. Similarly, it needed accelerated development of natural resources and manufacturing. The government was a direct beneficiary of private prosperity insofar as that prosperity reflected genuine national economic development and political stability; however, it soon became evident that the prosperity of some groups came at the expense of others. Having fostered industries with subsidies of various kinds, both the national and state governments had to contend with political and social problems, such as economic instability, deceptive business practices, and the growth of monopolies, that were directly attributable to the activities of the groups they originally supported. Moreover, economic change in areas that did not involve initial government subsidy created similar problems on such a broad scale that only the national government could deal with them effectively. The development of national monopolies in such industries as oil, steel, public utilities, and transportation created inevitable difficulties for small business, labor, agriculture, and the general consumer. This led to group conflict, which was transferred to governmental bodies at all levels. On the one hand governments were faced with a demand for new controls over the private economic sphere, and on the other they were pressured by very powerful and wealthy groups to maintain *laissez faire*. The net result was the establishment of limited government control of the economy during the latter part of the nineteenth century, and the way was paved for the far more extensive regulation that was to come later.

*Development of the Railroads* · An excellent illustration of the way in which nineteenth century American government became involved both in the promotion and regulation of the economy is provided by the development of the railroads.[3] This industry presented the most serious problems to government control in the century. The railroads received probably the greatest single subsidy ever given by the government to private enterprise, with the possible exception of present-day defense expenditure. The basis of the subsidy was typical: a national transportation system was needed, and there was not enough capital from private sources to develop railroads within the time felt to be necessary. The government embarked upon a program which eventually cost it one hundred and fifty-eight million acres of land. Some railroads received truly extraordinary grants: the Northern Pacific obtained forty-four million acres, while the Santa Fe, the Union Pacific, and the Central and Southern Pacific received over seventeen million acres each. In addition, other government help was given at both the national and state levels, including loans, tax

3. For information concerning the activities of the railroads in the nineteenth century see Samuel Eliot Morison and Henry Steele Commager, *The Growth of the American Republic* (5th ed., New York: Oxford University Press, 1962), II, chap. vii.

relief, protection from competitors, and outright grants of money. The entire industry, which came to dominate large sections of the country, was developed as a result of such incentives. Once established, it retained intimate contacts with government, particularly Congress and state legislatures, to ensure continued prosperity. As is generally the case with government subsidies, there were beneficial side-effects from the building of the railroads. Employment was provided for tens of thousands of workers, including many new immigrants. The development of a national transportation system pushed back the frontier and led directly to a national communications network.

Although the railroads made an enormous contribution to the country, they also began to abuse their dominant economic power in the decades following the Civil War. In some instances their freight rates were so high that the farmers, who could ship by no other means, burned their crops rather than submit to the roads. Generally there was little the roads did not do to take advantage of their semi-monopolistic position: discriminatory rates; rebates to powerful shippers; payoffs to state legislators; free passes to all who had influence; high rates in areas where there was no competition coupled with low rates in competitive locations, and so on. Inevitably demands were made, especially by the agrarian West, to curb these abuses. An analysis of the development of regulation of the railroads provides a basis for understanding the causes and problems of national regulation in general, for the regulatory mechanism, devised first for the railroads, set the pattern of future regulation in many other industries.

*The Failure of State Regulation of the Railroads* · Both before and after the Civil War the states attempted in various ways to curb the increasing abuses of the railroads, but their failure to do so reflected their general inability to exercise sufficient power to control industries which were national in scope. Why were the states unable to meet the challenge of effective economic regulation? First, there was the inherent defect in state regulation of powerful national industries: the problems and approaches of individual states differed, and such regulatory patterns as emerged necessarily lacked uniformity. Second, it was particularly easy for the railroads, as it was later for other powerful groups, to dominate state legislatures, executives, and the special regulatory commissions that were set up throughout the country. These commissions in some instances had initial rate-making and adjudicative power, as in the case of the powerful Illinois Board of Railroad and Warehouse Commissioners, created in 1871. In Illinois, there was strong agrarian support from the Granger movement for strict control of railroads and subsidiary operations. So strong was the feeling against the railroads there that elaborate provisions for control were written into the state constitution, adopted in 1870. Third, apart from isolated examples of strong state regulation, the vast majority of states failed to implement the necessary government control.

An additional obstacle to effective regulation faced by the states, and later by the national government, was the attitude of the courts. At the end of the nineteenth century and during much of the twentieth, the judiciary was generally unsympathetic to the goals of economic regulation. The problem of legislative removal of the jurisdiction of the courts from regulatory fields occurred later, particularly at the national level. Initially the so-called "Granger laws," establishing the right of the government to regulate private property in the public interest, were upheld in the historic case, *Munn v. Illinois* (1877), which specifically involved Illinois constitutional and statutory provisions regulating railroads. In the course of his opinion, Chief Justice Waite justified public regulation on the basis that private property affected with a public interest ceases to be private. Further, he stated that "property does become clothed with a public interest when used in a manner to make it of public consequence, and affect the community at large. When, therefore, one devotes his property to a use in which the public has an interest, he, in effect, grants to the public an interest in that use, and must submit to be controlled by the public for the common good, to the extent of the interest he has thus created." [4] It seemed that there was not going to be any serious constitutional obstacle in the path of state regulation.

Although the Supreme Court at the time of the *Munn* case supported the general idea of government control of industries affected with a public interest, a serious constitutional doubt was

4.  94 U.S. 113, 126 (1877).

soon raised as to the validity of state regulation over those portions of an industry engaged in *interstate* commerce. An indication of future developments came in 1877, the same year as the
*Munn* case, when the Court decided *Peik v. Chicago and North-
western Railway Co.*[5] The issue in this case was whether or not
the state of Wisconsin could regulate an interstate carrier. The
Court held that "until Congress acts in reference to the relations
of this company to interstate commerce, it is certainly within the
power of Wisconsin to regulate its fares, etc., so far as they are
of domestic concern. With the people of Wisconsin this company
has domestic relations. Incidentally, these may reach beyond
the State. But certainly, until Congress undertakes to legislate
for those who are without the State, Wisconsin may provide for
those within, even though it may indirectly affect those without."[6] In this case the issue was joined, and the proponents of
state regulation won; however, the *Peik* decision, like many before it left no doubt that where Congress chose to act in areas
involving interstate commerce it preempted the field.[7]

The Supreme Court became more conservative in the decade
of the eighties. In 1886 its decision in *Wabash, St. Louis & Pacific
Ry. Co. v. Illinois* [8] essentially overruled its previous opinions in
the *Peik* and *Munn* cases by holding that any firm engaged in
interstate commerce could not be regulated by the states through
which it passed. This, the Court held, was prohibited by the
commerce clause, which gave Congress the exclusive right to
regulate interstate commerce. This prohibition against state regulation did not apply to transportation solely within the boundaries
of a state, provided it was not connected in any way with interstate commerce. But there was little that needed regulation that
fell within the intrastate category; thus the *Wabash* decision
nullified all of the efforts that the states had made to regulate the
railroads. Further, the scope of this decision led to a preclusion
of state regulation in other needed areas, such as antitrust control, for it was almost a foregone conclusion that the most imperative government regulation would involve interstate firms.

5. 94 U.S. 164 (1887).
6. *Ibid.*, at 178.
7. For an early decision along these lines see *Gibbons v. Ogden,* 9
Wheaton 1 (1824).
8. 118 U.S. 557 (1886).

The economy of the United States was developing on a national scale, and state regulation was not only precluded on a constitutional basis by the Supreme Court, but also because of the evident failure of those state controls that had been established.

The obvious failure of the states led directly to the establishment of the Interstate Commerce Commission (ICC) in 1887. In many other areas it was not until the New Deal period that a recognition of a similar inadequacy of state regulation, coupled with a pressing need for national standards, led to the establishment of many new agencies patterned on the model of the ICC.

## THE FIRST REGULATORY AGENCY—THE INTERSTATE COMMERCE COMMISSION (1887)

The establishment of the ICC represented a historic step in the development of American bureaucracy.[9] It is important to note, first of all, that Congress decided to place regulatory power in the hands of a *commission,* i.e., an administrative agency, in order to cope with the problems of regulation of a national industry. Further, this Commission, although under the partial direction of the Secretary of the Interior until 1889, was *independent* in various ways of the President, Congress, and, later on, the courts. At the time of the creation of the ICC there had been a long history of state commissions; therefore the ICC was not entirely a revolutionary approach to economic regulation. Initially the most important change was the transference of the concept of commission regulation from the state to the national level.

In spite of the established tradition of state regulatory commissions, there was a sharp division of opinion in Congress, particularly between the Senate and the House, concerning whether or not a commission could handle the regulatory job that needed to be done. The term *administrative* was not applied to the ICC initially, and, as we shall see, it was not until the first decade of the twentieth century that this agency was recognized as something unique in government.

Why did Congress finally decide to adopt a commission form

9. For a comprehensive study of the independent regulatory commissions see Robert E. Cushman, *The Independent Regulatory Commissions* (New York: Oxford University Press, 1941).

of regulation in 1887? There can be no definite answer to this question. To some extent it was simply that the Senate proponents of the plan were able, through various types of political maneuvering, to get the bill passed. The House as a whole never thoroughly approved of the scheme, and in fact the whole idea was finally adopted only at the final conference stage, when representatives of both the House and the Senate met to iron out their differing points of view. Once the conference committee had agreed, the House was compelled to go along with the plan because of pressure for regulation from various groups and the public generally. No further delay would be tolerated.

Although the establishment of the ICC was at least in part accidental, many cogent arguments were advanced by those favoring the plan.[10] These ideas reflected much of what was later to become generally accepted as the theoretical basis of and justification for administrative regulation. First, the ICC was accepted as a more feasible regulatory body than Congress. From the very beginning it was recognized that the ability of a commission to specialize would give it more expert knowledge than could be possessed by all but a small handful of Congressmen. Further, a permanent commission could provide more continuity of public policy than an elected body. For this reason the ICC Commissioners were initially appointed by and with the advice and consent of the Senate for a term of six years, which was later increased to seven. It was expected that many Commissioners would be reappointed, and in many instances this has happened, with the result that continuity of service has been far greater than might appear from the minimum legal tenure. The staff of the agency, endowed with significant power, also was seen as a permanent force. At the time the ICC was created it was not generally expected to become an independent force in the exercise of legislative or judicial functions. In both these areas it was to act more in the capacity of an advisory body to Congress on the one hand and the judiciary on the other. The ICC was to inform Congress of needed legislation, but it was to be within the exclusive domain of Congress to determine what policies would be enacted. With respect to specific implementation the Commission depended for enforcement upon the courts. It soon became

10. These arguments may be found in *Ibid.*, pp. 19–65.

evident that *without the ability to exercise legislative and judicial power on an independent basis the ICC would never become an effective regulatory body.* This point is particularly emphasized because it is fundamental to an understanding of the evolution of the regulatory process. The history of the ICC illustrates this evolution, for beginning in the first decade of the twentieth century, it was strengthened by a number of congressional acts to provide it with independent legislative and judicial power.

Another reason for the adoption of the commission form of regulation resulted from the need for a *partisan* body to represent non-railroad interests. Today there is a very strong feeling that regulatory bodies should be *impartial,* particularly in their exercise of the judicial function (see Chapter 3). But the ICC and many similar bodies in other fields were purposely created to take punitive actions against the regulated industry. Partisanship, however, was not to be based upon political parties. In fact the need to avoid political favoritism was one of the most important justifications of a commission independent of presidential control, for the President is the leader of his party. Many Congressmen objected to establishing such a commission because they felt that it would not be partisan enough. This group favored a strict statute in which comprehensive regulatory standards would be defined in minute detail, with the courts designated as the primary bodies through which enforcement would be achieved. The actual Interstate Commerce Act of 1887 defined criteria for the Commission far more carefully than later regulatory statutes; nevertheless a large amount of discretion was still to remain with the ICC because the enabling Act contained such imprecise phrases as "just and reasonable." Moreover, the ICC did not have to enforce the law. Weak enforcement could mean nullification, the proponents of strong regulation argued, and in this they were correct.

Another important reason for vesting regulatory power in a commission was the highly *experimental* nature of the area of regulation. Despite the varied tradition of state regulation of the railroads there was not enough precedent to enable Congress to formulate anything but the roughest outlines of policy. Because of the experimental nature of the field the Commission was to advise Congress on needed legislation, and the presumption was that the experience of the ICC would weigh heavily in favor of congressional acceptance of its proposals.

The area of railroad regulation was not only experimental, it was highly volatile. Policy requirements would change from one period to the next; thus it would be impossible for Congress to keep up with the requirements for regulation even if it so desired. An administrative agency would be constantly in touch, and would be able to adjust regulatory policy in line with current problems and needs. Although these changes in policy were at first to be accomplished by Congress at the insistence of the ICC, the Commission was soon to become largely independent as a policy body.

Proponents of the ICC also pointed out that it would provide machinery for the reconciliation of disputes within the railroad industry, and the industry itself, suffering from cutthroat competition, supported this plea. In other industries it became quite common for the firms directly affected to support regulatory commissions, because they saw the commissions as a device to bring order into their relationships with competitors. Needless to say reputable businesses that operated with integrity in relation to their customers particularly favored regulation that would put an end to unfair competition. Moreover, as the economy became more interdependent it was not difficult to find strong political support for these new agencies, because business practices in one industry had repercussions throughout the country.

Although there were great hopes for the ICC in 1887, the Commission was unable to provide effective regulation as it lacked final legislative and adjudicative power. The enforcement power still resided in the judiciary. The courts insisted on reviewing Commission orders to such an extent that they were in effect substituting their judgment for that of the agency. The railroads soon saw that they could easily obstruct the ICC by appealing continuously to the courts. They even withheld evidence from the Commission on the accurate assumption that when they brought new evidence to the attention of the judiciary, on review the courts would insist on a *de novo* trial. The conservative leanings of the judiciary during the last decade of the nineteenth century essentially resulted in nullification of the powers of the ICC. The abuses of the railroads, however, continued virtually unchecked, and strong political pressure was brought to bear at the turn of the century to remedy the situation by strengthening the Commission and freeing it from the judicial hobble. Action was finally taken with the passage of the Hepburn Act of 1906, which gave the Commission final rate-making power subject to judicial review upon complaint of the carriers; thus rates established by the ICC were to become effective immediately without the need for prior judicial approval. This had the result of shifting the burden of proof upon the carriers if they wished to challenge an agency ruling. The powers of the Commission were extended at various times after the passage of the Hepburn Act, and by 1920 it was beginning to assume comprehensive regulatory authority.

Because of the debacle of the railroads in World War I, when the government took them over to avoid a complete breakdown in rail transportation, and their increasing problems resulting from the depression, it was recognized that the previous picture of a dominant and healthy industry was fading. The functions of the ICC began to shift from those which related to control in the public interest, that is, punitive actions, to those designed to foster a healthy industry, namely, promotional functions. This meant essentially that regulation in the public interest, as redefined, became equated to regulation in the interests of the railroads. This shift also reflected changing patterns of political support, which led to Commission reliance upon the very interests it was supposed to control for the necessary political support to maintain itself as an independent agency in the bureaucratic structure.

## EXPANSION OF THE INDEPENDENT
## REGULATORY COMMISSIONS

Starting in the second decade of the twentieth century regulatory commissions, analogous to the ICC, were established to control and promote various industries. The same pattern of development prevailed, and the reasons for the creation of these agencies in additional fields corresponded to those which led to the development of a strong and independent ICC. Although the railroad industry was the first to become national in character and impact, powerful national industries soon developed in other areas that required some form of regulation at the national rather than the state level. The same failure of the states to provide effective regulation that was apparent with regard to the rail-road industry was evident in other fields. In some cases, of course, state regulatory agencies developed concurrently with their national counterparts; however, their powers necessarily were limited to intrastate matters.

At the national level the ICC provided a precedent for the establishment of similar commissions in new fields. The necessary increase in the powers of the ICC at the beginning of the twentieth century because of judicial nullification of legislative purpose convinced many that the best organizational structure for effective regulation was the independent agency combining significant legislative and judicial functions. The more powerful these agencies were to be, the more important a certain degree of independence seemed. Their independence of the President and to a degree also of Congress did not prevent the agencies from implementing the law in terms of the political interests involved. These interests, however, were not generally associated with the parties, but involved both private and public interest groups which exerted pressure for the implementation of policies to their particular advantage. The agencies, then, were in many cases perfectly free at first to be partisan, in the sense of favoring one group of interests over another, as long as such partisanship did not relate directly to the major political parties.

At the time of the establishment of the ICC the most clearly articulated interests, those of the agrarian mid-West and West, called for administration of the Act of 1887 in their favor. The railroads, caught off guard at first, soon remedied that situation by using the courts as destructive instruments during the first decade of the administration of the Act. By the time later agencies, such as the Federal Trade Commission were established, industry interests supported the idea of commission regulation as long as the agencies became no more than arbiters of industry disputes. No matter what an agency did it would necessarily be supporting one set of interests over another.

Apart from the breakdown of state regulation, and the precedent of the ICC, new regulatory agencies were created because of needs of specialization, knowledge, continuity of public policy,

and so forth, all of which had been raised in the past by proponents of the independent commission form of organization.
Further, in virtually every case these additional regulatory agencies were established as a result of political pressure for some
form of national control, arising directly from economic problems associated with the industries concerned. The ICC was
created because of agrarian pressure; similarly, group demands
led to the creation of such agencies as the Federal Reserve Board
in 1913, the Federal Trade Commission in 1914, the Federal
Power Commission in 1920, and numerous New Deal agencies.
The political support for these agencies was not always as well
organized as that behind the ICC; however, no agency was created
in an atmosphere detached from the political process.

The establishment of virtually every regulatory agency was
considered a revolutionary step by those directly affected; therefore, extraordinary political pressure was frequently directed at
Congress to prevent the passage of regulatory statutes. The
statutes were finally passed because proponents of the plans were
able to muster sufficient political strength to overcome the opposition of powerful groups in the industry. Not all members of the
proposed areas of regulation were opposed to government controls, and some sought such regulation to provide protection
against detrimental competitive practices.

It can not be too strongly emphasized, then, that the process
leading to the establishment of administrative agencies is *highly
political,* and administrative functions and organization are essentially determined by political factors. No administrative agency
in the American system, which supports pluralism and democratic participation (however limited), has been created on a
permanent basis by governmental fiat. Agencies must have strong
political support from the community itself, whether from groups,
political parties, or individuals, in order to become established
and to survive.

Finally, it should be noted that in the twentieth century, a
great expansion in the scope and responsibilities of government
at all levels occurred. This culminated in the New Deal, which
solidified the idea that the national government should be responsible for the welfare of the nation in numerous fields. This
idea was not new, of course, but the New Deal led directly to an

acceptance of the responsibility of government for economic regulation by both political parties. Bipartisan acknowledgment of such responsibility was finally achieved with the Eisenhower administration, and although there are dissenters in both parties, Republicans and Democrats as a whole accept the national regulatory process. The Presidency, crystallizing an always nebulous public opinion, has provided additional political support for the expansion of bureaucracy generally. This has led some to look upon the administrative process as a primary instrument for the achievement of democratic goals, in terms of implementing the mandates of the people through the President.

## THE REGULATORY PROCESS IN EXECUTIVE DEPARTMENTS

Although we have concentrated on the expansion of the independent regulatory agencies, it is a mistake to think of bureaucracy solely in such terms. In many areas of domestic policy formulation these agencies exercise the most important control; however, different economic and political needs have produced administrative agencies exercising vast legislative and adjudicative powers that do not fit the classification "independent regulatory commission." Many executive agencies perform regulatory functions as part of a broader responsibility. Administrative functions, divided into legislative, judicial, and executive categories, are exercised by all types of agencies; however, at the same time agencies may differ with respect to the reasons for their establishment, their principal goals, and organizational structures. These factors are largely determined by political forces which lead to the creation of particular agencies and provide a basis for continuing support.

If one views the executive branch as a whole, it becomes evident that most of the departments exercise significant regulatory power. The reasons for locating such power within these departments are similar to those that led to the establishment of the independent regulatory commissions. Regulatory functions are usually performed by separate agencies within departments, and unlike their commission counterparts they are generally responsible for the regulation of a narrow aspect of private activity, not an entire industry. The Department of Agriculture is a particularly vivid example of many subordinate groups (the Commodity Credit Corporation, Commodity Exchange Authority, Farmers Home Administration) engaged in regulation.

Most agencies exercising regulatory functions within departments possess both legislative and judicial power. Given the similarity of the functions they possess to those of the independent regulatory commissions it is natural to ask why different organizational patterns were employed in different areas. In part the answer is that there is not necessarily any logic to organizational standards in American bureaucracy, or at least not enough logic that people will always agree that a given form of organization should be used when certain functions are to be exercised. Perhaps a better answer would be that many regulatory fields are relatively narrow, and are more easily and conveniently put under the jurisdiction of a department that possesses responsibility for a broad but related area. There is also the fact that in many of the major regulatory fields Congress likes to consider the agency established as an arm of the legislature, not of the President; hence, the independent designation is used. In both congressional and administrative circles the independent regulatory agencies are frequently termed "arms of Congress." Congress is not so concerned about some relatively narrow regulatory areas, and is perfectly willing to place them within the purview of the President by locating them within executive departments.

Political demands also dictate the location of these agencies. When the independent commissions were established there was enough support both within and without Congress to keep them outside departmental jurisdiction. On the other hand in many instances in which agencies were established to function in a field related to a politically powerful department, there was a strong demand from that department to place the new agency under its control. For example, many new regulatory needs were recognized in the field of agriculture during the 'thirties. By that time the Department of Agriculture was well entrenched as one of the most powerful members of the executive branch; therefore it was virtually impossible to found new agencies in the agricultural field outside the Department. The process of location of agencies is as political as that involved in their establishment. Departments without strong political support in the form of interest groups are likely to be bypassed in the placement of new agencies. The State Department provides an excellent example of this.

## EXPANSION OF BUREAUCRACY INTO OTHER AREAS

*Department of Defense* · American bureaucracy has also developed significant power in many areas that can not be classified as regulatory. First, there has been a tremendous increase in the powers and responsibilities of the Defense Department. This agency, which can not really be considered as a whole but only in terms of subgroups, employs over one-half of all the *civilians* in federal service. Its appropriation amounts to close to sixty per cent of the national budget—over fifty billion dollars. Its responsibilities, shared with the President and Congress, encompass no less than the security of the nation. In the pursuit of this goal the Department exercises powers that affect everyone in the nation directly or indirectly. The reasons for this extraordinary location of power (and we shall see later that the Department is frequently autonomous) are historical, international, and technological.

Congress and the President were to share the "war power" under the Constitution—the former having the power to raise and support armies and declare war, the latter being Commander-in-Chief of the armed forces. Numerous treatises have been written to describe how Congress has lost most of its power in this field to the President because of the latter's superior sources of information and ability to respond rapidly to international events. Although the powers of the President are extraordinary, the military arm will always possess and attempt to employ for its own purposes a high degree of independence. The same factors that led to presidential supremacy over Congress in this area also supported the increasing role of the Defense Department as an autonomous policy force.

The dominant power of the Defense Department, linked with that of the President, has arisen because of the increasing involvement of the United States in the world community, and because of repeated crises that have placed primary emphasis upon the importance of defense and military affairs since the beginning of World War II. At times in the past, as in the Civil War period, the branches of military assumed powers which gave them more than the usual strength, especially in combination with that of the President, over Congress and the courts. Before World War II, however, the military was unable to determine policy for more than brief periods of time. In fact, an examination of congressional-military relations during this period would reveal a dominant Congress turning down repeated and varied military requests. As long as the business of defense was of manageable proportions, and in the absence of strong public demand for stringent measures of military preparedness, it was not difficult to keep the military branches under control.

The generally isolationist attitude in the United States prior to World War II prevented any sustained political support for the military arm of government. Neither Congress, private interest groups, nor the President felt it necessary to establish a large and powerful military branch. In fact, during the period of the 'thirties it was the President who supported substantial reductions in the military budget, not Congress; and beginning in 1936, Congress *added* funds to the budget requests made by the President for the War Department in the face of the continued opposition of the Bureau of the Budget (the President's principal budgetary staff agency). Beginning in 1941, it was common practice for Congress to give the War Department as much money as it initially requested, and in some cases more than it wanted; however, the general practice of the Bureau of the Budget was to cut War Department requests. Beginning with World War II the military branches began to use Congress and private interest groups as a lever against presidential domination.

World War II brought about a change in the relative power position of the military branches to other agencies and departments of the government. Problems involved in military policy formulation became increasingly complex, and in many areas these tended to isolate Congress, and to a lesser extent the President, as effective instruments of control. From time to time presidential decisions have an important effect upon defense policy. Nowhere is this better illustrated than in the immediate and far-reaching changes implemented by President Kennedy after he came into office.[11] However, the Defense Department, which is now a per-

11. See William P. Gerberding, "American Foreign Policy: The First Year of the Kennedy Administration," *American Government Annual 1962–1963* (New York: Holt, Rinehart and Winston, 1962), pp. 99–101.

manent and powerful force in government, necessarily controls much of the information upon which decisions at a higher level are made. In this way it shapes the nature of the policies finally adopted. Advancements in military technology have made the defense field one in which great knowledge is needed to comprehend the factors involved in decision making. This development always results in an increase in bureaucratic autonomy.

The Defense Department, then, as a result of World War II and the succeeding "Cold War" has been put on a permanent basis. Military technology, as well as contributing to the autonomy of the Department, also has resulted in the necessity of establishing and maintaining a permanent armaments industry of gigantic proportions, which in turn has provided a continuing basis of political support for the Department itself. In the past the United States has always been able to supply the necessary military weapons to our forces after hostilities started. This could easily be accomplished as long as weapons systems were relatively conventional and capable of rapid design and production; however, the experience of World War II, in which this country was caught in a state of inadequate preparedness, coupled with the increasingly complex nature of weapons systems, forced the development of both an administrative department and private planning and production facilities that could provide continuous military research and development. One can not imagine this country today, for example, attempting to develop guided missiles spontaneously after the beginning of hostilities. The very nature of military technology contributes to the maintenance of a powerful Defense Department.

The development of bureaucratic power is also notable outside the regulatory realm in benefit agencies, public corporations (which may possess regulatory functions), certain staff agencies, and agencies involved in what are essentially public or interagency service functions (e.g., the Post Office Department, which possesses adjudicative and rule making functions in addition to its service functions). Although these agencies are not "regulatory" in the sense in which that term is applied to the independent regulatory commissions, they perform regulatory functions to varying degrees. The growth of bureaucracy in all these areas reflects the increasing demands that are placed upon the national government to assume responsibility for policy development and regulation.

*Benefit Agencies* · In the benefit field, for example, the primary agencies of importance are the Social Security Administration, particularly the Bureau of Old-Age and Survivors Insurance, and the Veterans Administration (VA), both of which were developed to meet public demands for benefits. The VA is of considerable importance because of the large number of citizens who served in the armed forces during the latter part of the nineteenth and in the twentieth centuries. At present this agency dispenses over five billion dollars in benefits each year and affects approximately eighty million persons, in particular twenty-two million veterans and their families. The Social Security Administration is of equal importance, and dispenses over ten billion dollars in benefits each year. It is a mistake to think of the work of agencies such as these as being merely routine; in fact a great number of discretionary decisions are made by administrators in these agencies which affect in a very substantial manner individual rights and obligations. The principal function of both the VA and the Social Security Administration is adjudication—the application of general rules in specific cases. The funds for these immense enterprises are supplied in the case of the VA through general taxation and with regard to social security mostly through special payroll taxes. It should be pointed out that the VA is an independent agency and subject to very little outside control; the BOASI is within the Department of Health, Education, and Welfare.

*Government Corporations* · The government corporation is an interesting administrative device. It was virtually unknown before the New Deal era, but since that time, and particularly during World War II, it has come to be of importance in the bureaucratic structure. Originally government corporations were given a great deal more freedom of action, especially in the fiscal area, than regular departments and agencies. They were set up to accomplish relatively specific tasks, such as insuring and extending credit to banking facilities (Reconstruction Finance Corporation, Federal Deposit Insurance Corporation), regional development (Tennessee Valley Authority), or developing raw materials, for example, to meet specific needs during wartime. At first many of these corporations were much like their private counterparts, operating with independent funds given initially by Congress but sustained through the corporation revenues. But in 1945 the Government Corporation Control Act was passed which, while preserving some of the previous independence of the corporations, sought to make them more accountable to Congress and the President. Government corporations, which were set up at first on an *ad hoc* basis to meet specific problems, have become a permanent part of American bureaucracy. Although there are only about a dozen today, they exercise functions vital to the community as a whole as well as to the particular areas they control.

*Staff Agencies* · Finally, a brief note should be taken of the development of staff agencies. In this category fall those groups that provide facilities for planning and coordination, and act principally in an advisory capacity to operating departments. All agencies, of course, have their staff divisions; in addition to intra-agency staff groups several significant agencies have developed whose sole purpose is to provide operating departments with planning assistance. In particular the Bureau of the Budget and the National Security Council should be mentioned; the former is a budgetary and legislative coordinating and planning agency, the latter advises the President on major national security problems. This type of bureaucracy arose in response to the need to provide adequate staff facilities and to coordinate bureaucratic operations in the sprawling maze of agencies.

## The Constitutional and Political Aspects of Bureaucratic Organization

In terms of the impact the bureaucracy has upon the governmental process as a whole, it is important to point out the way in which political considerations intrude into its organization as well as its functions.

### CONSTITUTIONAL FACTORS AFFECTING ADMINISTRATIVE ORGANIZATION

The Constitution has profoundly affected the structure of American bureaucracy; it explains in many instances differences between administrative organization in America and many other countries. This statement may seem, at first, inconsistent with the discussion of the Constitution in Chapter 1, in which it was pointed out that our constitutional system was necessarily constructed without thought to the kind of bureaucracy we have today. If bureaucracy is not mentioned in the Constitution in any important way, how has the resulting system of government affected bureaucratic organization?

First, the Constitution was actually ambiguous as to who was going to control the small executive branch of the new Republic. This ambiguity stemmed from the general separation of powers rather than from specific provisions designed to fragment control of the executive branch. In fact Alexander Hamilton articulated a concept of presidential responsibility for the administrative branch, as it was then known, in *The Federalist,* although his definition of administrative activity was confined to "mere execution" and "executive details," and in no way encompassed what was to develop later. In *Federalist 72,* after defining administration in this narrow way, Hamilton stated:

. . . The persons, therefore, to whose immediate management these different [administrative] matters are committed, ought to be considered as the assistants or deputies of the chief magistrate, and on this account, they ought to derive their offices from his appointment, at least from his nomination, and ought to be subject to his superintendence. This view of the subject will at once suggest to us the intimate connection between the duration of the executive magistrate in office and the stability of the system of administration. To reverse and undo what has been done by a predecessor, is very often considered by a successor as the best proof he can give of his own capacity and desert; and in addition to this propensity, where the alteration has been the result of public choice, the person substituted is warranted in supposing that the dismission of his predecessor has proceeded from a dislike to his measures. . . .

In other words, the President is to be responsible for administrative action as long as he is in office. These statements of Hamilton, combined with his expressed belief in the necessity of vigor, energy, and *unity* in the Presidency, led the early administrative management theorists to say that it was the intention of the constitutional system to place the entire administrative branch under the President. Whether or not this was, or might have been, the intention of those who framed the Constitution had they foreseen the nature of bureaucratic development, the fact is that the system they constructed supported in many particulars bureaucratic organization and functions independent of the President. It was the role they assigned *Congress* in relation to administration that assured this result, as well as the general position Congress was to occupy in the governmental system.

Let us, briefly, juxtapose the powers of Congress and the President over the bureaucracy as they are derived from the Constitution. First, with respect to the organization of bureaucracy, Congress retains the primary power. It may create and destroy agencies, and it determines where they are to be located, in the executive branch and outside it. This is one of the key powers of Congress regarding administrative organization, enabling it to create a highly autonomous bureaucracy. In addition, Congress has the power of appropriation, and in this way too it is able to exercise a great deal of control over the administrative arm. Congress can not only set up an administrative agency on an independent basis, but it can see to it that the agency remains independent. Moreover, Congress has the power to define exactly what the agency may or may not do, that is, its general jurisdiction. Finally, the Constitution gives Congress the power to interfere in certain presidential appointments, which are to be "by and with the advice and consent of the Senate." Congress may, of course, extend the sharing of the appointive power when it sets up new agencies. As a result of these powers, Congress has virtually complete authority to structure the administrative branch and determine where formal lines of accountability shall be placed. It may or may not decide to let the President exercise various types of controls.

Turning to the powers of the President over the bureaucracy, especially as they relate to bureaucratic structure and lines of control, it is evident that the Constitution gives him a relatively small role. Not only did the Constitution purposely pit Congress against the President in the governmental system generally, it gave Congress greater reign over the bureaucracy. One of the primary purposes of the constitutional system is to motivate the branches of government to oppose each other; therefore Congress and the President are adversaries. The effect of this upon bureaucratic structure is that Congress does not wish to increase the President's power over administrative agencies any more than necessary. For this reason there is a positive desire on the part of Congress to give many agencies independence. Simply because an agency is engaged in administrative functions does not mean that it should be placed within the executive branch, according to many past and present members of Congress. This view is emphasized because administrative *functions* are not so much executive as they are *legislative* and *judicial*. Insofar as they are legislative, it is natural for Congress to consider the agencies as an extension of itself; insofar as they are judicial, Congress feels in many instances that administrative independence is desirable, to avoid partisan influence over judicial proceedings.

The Constitution, then, has left a great deal of ambiguity regarding exactly where agencies are to be located, and to whom they are to be accountable. Although there is little doubt that Hamilton might have wished the bureaucracy to be under presidential control, the system established did not indicate this. Thus, to say that it is the constitutional responsibility of the President to control the administrative branch is not accurate, because he was not given the tools to do so. Considering many agencies as arms of Congress is as much in accord with the Constitution as maintaining that the bureaucracy is the responsibility of the President.

Finally, federalism has had a profound effect on bureaucratic organization in that it has necessitated various devices to aid the administrative branch in carrying out its programs in areas involving federal-state cooperation. Frequently, for example, federal and state agencies must cooperate in program implementation if national policy is to be effective. In addition to other factors such as geography, economic dispersion, and sectionalism, such cooperation has fostered a decentralized federal bureaucracy, and an emphasis upon field organizations. In turn, this development has caused various problems of control in the federal bureaucracy, for a field agency always has a certain amount of autonomy resulting not only from such factors as distance, but also from local political support for program implementation that may or may not accord with central directives and policy. The fact that the states and their agencies possess a great deal of independent power under our constitutional system explains the existence of a variety of organizational patterns in the bureaucracy, as well as many problems of congressional or presidential control of the administrative branch.

The effect of the Constitution is to fragment the bureaucracy. Lines of control are blurred, organizational patterns are diverse, and in general unity is absent. The Constitution has fragmented our political system generally, and the bureaucracy is no exception. In the same way that we have pluralism in our society, we have it throughout the government and in the administrative branch in particular. If the Constitution had structured our government as a whole to operate on a principle of fusion of power between executive and legislative branches, and had possibly provided a unitary rather than a federal form in relation to the country as a whole, the bureaucracy, reflecting this unity, would be more cohesive both in terms of organization and operation.

## POLITICAL FACTORS SHAPING AMERICAN BUREAUCRATIC STRUCTURE

The Constitution alone is not responsible for lack of unity in our political system, and a change in the constitutional system would not by itself provide a cure. The great variety of interests throughout the country is reflected politically, and results in the exertion of diverse pressures on the bureaucracy by groups of all kinds. This kind of pressure is made more significant because of the lack of administrative unity and because the bureaucracy is deeply involved in the policy process. There is no single focal point of control for the administrative branch, and the way is cleared for disjointed control by interest groups in proportion to their political power.

Political pressure is largely responsible for the creation of administrative agencies in the first place, as we have seen; in addition once an agency has been established it begins to develop what is in effect a *constituency*, that is, a number of groups and individuals over which it has, in some instances, jurisdiction, and with which it interacts in a variety of ways. In the broadest sense the constituency of an agency includes those groups, both governmental and nongovernmental, whose interests must be taken into account, and because they must be taken into account the agency is by definition responsible to its constituency. In terms of this definition, administrative constituencies include those private groups within the jurisdiction of the agency, congressional committees, other administrative agencies, the judiciary, and the Presidency. At this point we may assume that the "public" is subsumed within these designated groups composing the administrative constituency. Although at first statutory provisions have a lot to do with defining administrative constituencies, soon extra-legal factors come into play. Constituencies are fluid over a period of time, and in addition change as the issues requiring administrative decision change. There is always a core element of a constituency that can be identified as being relatively stable; however, the concept of administrative constituencies is dynamic, not static.

It is administrative constituencies that determine organizational patterns. The groups within constituencies must, of course, operate within our constitutional framework, and their attitudes are in part shaped by their role within the constitutional system. Not only do administrative constituencies determine structure, but the structure of an administrative agency should in the broadest sense be considered to include its constituency. Congressional and presidential constituencies are frequently considered an integral part of those institutions, and the same should apply to the administrative branch.

Administrative constituencies are composed of diverse groups with divergent attitudes. The agency is the focal point of the constituency structure, and it seeks to maintain a balance of political support over opposition. In any given situation, and in some cases generally, there will be interests opposed to particular agencies. Because they are in opposition does not, of course, affect the fact that they form part of the agency's constituency. This raises the question of why agencies respond to governmental and private interest groups in the process of making decisions. In some instances they are compelled to because of statutory mandates. For example, the statutes governing their activities may state that under certain circumstances the decisions of an agency are subject to judicial review. This type of provision immediately places the judiciary within the constituency of the agency involved, with respect to a particular decision making area. In a similar way statutes set up lines of control and authority from agencies to other administrative groups, to the President, and to Congress. The diversity of the constituencies of administrative agencies based upon statutory provisions stems in part from the ambiguity of constitutional provisions as to who is to control administrative activity.

Statutory provisions also help to define private constituencies for administrative agencies by setting up their jurisdiction. In other words, statutes define the areas over which agencies are to have control, and in this way the groups that will be affected by agency action are determined. These groups become part of the agency's constituency.

What groups oppose and what groups support administrative agencies? This, of course, depends upon a number of factors, including the constitutional and statutory position of the groups within the administrative constituency. Within the stable core of the constituency, agencies frequently have strong support from private groups in the industry that is being regulated, which in turn may be reflected in support from particular congressmen and congressional committees. In such instances the agencies tend to be relatively autonomous, regardless of the existence of legal lines of authority from the agency to superiors in the administrative branch, such as the President or a department head. For example, the Army Corps of Engineers is placed by statute within the Department of the Army, which is in turn in the Defense Department. From a legal point of view the Corps is subject to control by the Secretary of the Army, the Secretary of Defense, and the President. Also, the President's authority over the Corps is strengthened by the constitutional provision making him Commander-in-Chief of the Armed Forces. From a statutory and constitutional standpoint nothing could be clearer than the fact that this administrative agency is subject to many lines of control from superiors. The fact is, however, that the Corps has developed exceptionally strong *political* support from outside groups, many of which have a local orientation that is reflected in Congress. Thus, Congress is intensely interested in preserving the Corps on an independent basis in order to enable it to act in congressional interests. The dominant forces in its constituency are private and congressional, and hence the decisions of the Corps are oriented in this direction.

Administrative agencies tend generally to act in accordance with the dominant interests in their constituency, and to some extent the attitude of the "constituents" towards the agency is determined by the extent to which they can influence its behavior. An agency, for example, which consistently acts in opposition to the private groups within its jurisdiction is likely to incur their wrath. This tends to be reflected in Congress and generally results in congressional opposition to the agency. If an agency is to survive it must be able to obtain enough political support from non-opposing groups to offset adversary groups. Such support may, and frequently does, come from the President and other administrative agencies. Both government and private allies are necessary to sustain most agencies, and rarely will there be significant government support unless there is private support.

Let us consider a further example of the way political interests affect organizational patterns. In 1962, the Interstate Commerce Commission, acting in its role as promoter of the private interests under its control, decided that in a number of cases the only effective way to promote a healthy railroad industry was to permit the establishment of quasi-monopolies in certain areas; hence it began to encourage railroad mergers. It was strongly supported in this move by certain groups in Congress, some of which in fact were criticizing the ICC for not having moved faster in this direction before. Congress, in 1948, exempted ICC decisions on mergers from the antitrust laws; thus the Commission had the legal authority to act without consulting with the Justice Department's Antitrust Division, which normally controls business mergers with the aid of the Federal Trade Commission.

With respect to the proposed railroad mergers numerous interests came into play: (1) the railroads themselves wanted as much freedom as possible to determine the conditions of mergers (the ICC has no power legally to force mergers); (2) certain groups in Congress, and part of the ICC staff felt that the ICC should take an active part in the determination of merger conditions, and the effects of particular mergers on the national railroads generally; (3) the mergers were generally opposed by railroad unions, because they feared substantial reductions in membership as a result of the greater efficiency and economy that would take place from the mergers; (4) many communities that faced reduced service after the mergers reacted unfavorably; (5) the Justice Department had not taken an official stand (it could act only in an advisory capacity in such cases), but it was opposed to the mergers because it felt that they violated the anti-trust laws. These were, and still are, the interests in the ICC's constituency. The Commission has not yet resolved the situation; but whatever it does will be in effect a compromise among these diverse interest groups. In legal terms the ICC is independent; in fact it must respond to political pressure, and remain in accord with the dominant interests in its constituency. Because of the powerful support the ICC usually receives from the railroads it is a safe guess that it will respond favorably to their merger proposals, and accept in large part the terms they offer.

## Conclusion

The political basis for the establishment and organization of the administrative branch should not be thought of as isolated from consideration of the *functions* of bureaucracy elaborated in Chapter 1, nor as unrelated to many of the problems that arise with regard to the constitutional role of bureaucracy. The organization of bureaucracy relates directly to the problem of control. The organizational patterns provide the environment within which administrative agencies perform legislative, executive, and judicial functions. Thus, for example, one of the justifications for the independent regulatory commission is that its independence gives it greater impartiality in the performance of judicial decision-making, a desirable goal to many theorists. Similarly, agencies are frequently thought appropriately placed within executive departments because their functions fit the "executive" category more than anything else.

The exercise of administrative functions involves several important problems. First, when administrative agencies formulate legislation, either through rule making or through direct influence on Congress, democratic theory requires at least limited control by the people. Congress as a whole does not control the bureaucracy, nor does the President. The question naturally posed is to what extent can the administrative branch, in terms of present organization, be considered democratic? In general it is possible to state as a minimum that the bureaucracy can be controlled from a variety of sources, which, when put together, constitute a form of democratic control. The fragmentation of administrative organization may preclude the possibility of control by any one governmental or nongovernmental group, but this does not prevent meaningful control entirely. The fact is that in the American system of government there is no cohesive majority and hence no possibility that one group will represent the "will of the people," whatever that term may mean. Bureaucratic organization is but a reflection of the pattern of American government; thus it may not be justified to criticize the bureaucracy because of its relatively autonomous position, and because of lack of unified control. The former is characteristic of all branches of government, and unity does not exist anywhere in the American system. In this regard the legislative functions of administrative agencies are in harmony with organizational patterns, i.e., administrative organization does not by itself prevent a proper performance of these functions insofar as democratic control is involved. This does not mean, of course, that there may not be other factors limiting adequate democratic control.

Second, administrative policy formulation necessitates some degree of planning and coordination. The proper nature of such planning and coordination is subject to debate, and there is little agreement about these areas in public administration. Criticisms have been made of the administrative process that the lack of central direction, either within agencies or from a source outside the bureaucracy, results in a serious lack of planning and coordination. Planning involves, and in the minds of many, necessitates, inter-agency coordination. The independence of agencies, often a statutory independence, acts as an impediment to the attainment of this goal. The Interstate Commerce Commission, for example, does not have to coordinate its activities with the Justice Department in the field of railroad mergers; hence it may frequently be working at cross purposes with the anti-trust division of the Justice Department. Agency constituencies, which determine to a large extent administrative decisions, differ and place different demands upon various agencies; this is the basic reason for the lack of agency coordination of policy. Administrative organization is not conducive to securing inter-agency cooperation.

There are other implications of agency organization that should be noted with regard to problems of policy formulation, planning, and coordination. The independent regulatory commissions have been accused of having organizational structures that place too many demands upon top agency officials in the adjudicative process, leaving them too little time for planning and proper policy formulation. Some observers have proposed a greater separation of legislative and judicial functions, the latter being delegated as much as possible to specialized groups within or outside the agencies, and the former left as the primary responsibility of agency heads and commissioners. The result would presumably be greater time for long range planning as top administrators become freed from the "details" of day-to-day administration. This proposed change in administrative organization was a central recommendation of a report made to President Kennedy in December of 1960.[12] Proposals of this kind relate directly to the problem of whether or not—or the extent to which—the judicial functions of administrative agencies can be separated from their legislative functions.

Third, in the area of administrative adjudication, we will see in the next chapter on administrative law that there are criteria for administrative justice that are thought by many to be essential to the maintenance of constitutional government. One criterion for the realization of due process of law is that the judge must be impartial in decision making. Agency organization frequently tends to orient decisions in the direction of particular constituencies, and sometimes in favor of particular constituents. Although the agencies may not be partisan in the sense of favoring one political party over another, they are highly political. This aspect of their organization does not foster detachment. It has led to recommendations for a stricter separation of functions within the agencies, and to proposals for the establishment of administrative courts that would be completely separated from the agencies

12. James M. Landis, *Report on Regulatory Agencies to the President-Elect* (committee print of the Subcommittee on Administrative Practice and Procedure of the Committee on the Judiciary, U.S. Senate, 86th Cong., 2nd Sess., 1960).

themselves to hear cases that normally arise within the agencies' jurisdiction.

Finally, with respect to the proper performance of many executive functions, there are those who feel that efficiency demands that the agencies be placed under some form of central control. The problems that arise in accounting and supply, for example, are quite different from those that are present in the legislative and judicial areas of administrative activity. Centralization, and even coordination, might seem clearly appropriate organizational devices to achieve goals of executive efficiency in the former, but are in fact far more questionable in the latter areas. To some extent the political aspects of public administration and administrative organization make the efficient management of executive details more difficult. This is assuming, for the moment, that "efficiency" is desirable in the executive field.

Administrative organization may or may not aid in the implementation of a given definition of what should constitute proper performance of administrative functions. The functions of administrative agencies fall into legislative, judicial, and executive categories. An organizational pattern that may facilitate one's definition of proper performance, say, in the legislative area may hinder the achievement of performance goals in the judicial or executive areas. The problem of relating, even in theory, functional goals with organization is difficult.

It has been suggested that the organizational patterns of American bureaucracy are more or less "set" in terms of our constitutional and political system. In other words, given our system of government it is very hard to see how bureaucratic organization can be substantially changed. This does not mean, of course, that particular agencies can not be moved about from one part of the organization to another; however, regardless of where agencies are located they will tend to act in terms of their constituencies, and the bureaucracy generally will present a picture of fragmented power. Any discussion of how administrative functions should be performed must recognize the organizational context of the bureaucracy and must take note of the fact that organization shapes the performance of function to a substantial degree. Many proposals for change in American bureaucracy recommend structuring the agencies in a way that is entirely unrealistic in terms of the political context within which they function.

# CHAPTER 3 Administrative Law and the Courts

THE VAGUENESS of congressional standards governing agency operation necessarily leaves a great deal of discretion in the hands of the administrative branch. Because of this it is generally accurate to think of the process of agency rule making as one of filling in the details of vague laws. The term "administrative law" embraces both the legislative and judicial aspects of administrative activity, because administrative agencies implement policy, or legislation, through a process of bringing and settling specific cases. Administrative law initially involves agency rule making, which is the establishment of regulations (laws) pertaining to the community and governing the activities of those groups falling within their jurisdiction. In terms of this definition administrative law becomes the law that is established by the administrative branch. Agency rules also govern internal administrative procedure, but for the moment we are interested only in rules that pertain to groups outside of the agencies themselves.

When administrative law is equated to agency legislation (or rules) it is generally referred to as "substantive law." Some idea of the volume of substantive agency legislation may be seen in the Code of Federal Regulations, which contains agency rules that have been previously published in the Federal Register. In the Code the agencies interpret for the public, and more specifically for the groups falling within their jurisdiction, the general standards established by Congress.

Apart from the substantive element in administrative law, there is an area which encompasses the procedures used by agencies in deciding cases and controversies, that is, administrative adjudication. The term "administrative law" is more frequently than not equated with it, and in fact there are many who feel that the procedural aspects of agency adjudication should be strictly separated from the role of the agencies in legislation, for essentially the same reasons that American constitutional practice separates legislative and judicial powers. This proposal for separation of functions, which was appropriate to the eighteenth and much of the nineteenth centuries, may not be feasible in terms of the present role of the bureaucracy in our constitutional system.

## The Nature of Administrative Adjudication

"Adjudication" refers to the specific disposition of a case and controversy, and may be contrasted with such terms as "law making" or "rule-making," that involve the formulation of general standards applicable to an entire community. These definitions are general; hence, they are always subject to qualification in particular circumstances. In other words, it is not always clear if a given governmental action is adjudication or legislation. Even the most learned judges have been confused on this point, not to mention those less expert in the nature of the law and legal procedure. In addition to being specific, adjudication and the exercise of judicial power is usually considered to be *final*, in that it is subject only to limited judicial review. Review of an initial adjudicative determination, regardless of whether it was made in the administrative process or by a court, is always carefully prescribed. This is clearly necessary; otherwise every judicial decision would have to be considered *de novo* if one of the parties requested it. Only certain questionable aspects of a judicial proceeding will be reviewed as a general rule. Specificity and finality, then, are the key attributes of adjudication.

Wherever judicial power is exercised there will always be policy considerations in the background. The real issue between administrative law and the various areas of law implemented by the judiciary is not whether policy should intrude upon the decision making process, but *what policy* is to be followed. The procedural policy that is adopted will shape the substantive policy followed, for it will determine those factors taken into account in the decision process. Because judicial procedure emphasizes individual interests, it tends to shape much of the policy the courts feel should be implemented. Administrative procedure is theoretically supposed to permit policy implementation beyond the demands of the most immediate and powerful interests, but this does not always work. The importance of administrative constituencies in the determination of the course of action taken by the bureaucracy was indicated in the previous chapter. The impact of these constituencies, however, may be somewhat distant from the immediate interests involved in a particular case. An administrative determination may be made on the basis of powerful interests that are frequently far removed from the immediate adjudicative process. Court procedure tends to relate the decision disposing of a particular matter to the most powerful immediate adversary, i.e., the party that makes the most effective case.

The initial context of administrative adjudication is determined by Congress in the various statutes that govern agency organization, jurisdiction, and procedure. Consider the typical congressional statutes that set up an administrative agency and define its powers. After designating the group or individual responsible for the implementation of the law, they outline in general terms the powers the agency is to possess, the procedures it is to employ in administering the law (which include both adjudication and rule making), and the extent of judicial review. Questions frequently arise about the limitations placed upon administrative agencies; whether there is judicial review of administrative decisions, whether the President controls the agencies, etc. The first place to look for an answer to these questions is in the enabling statutes, as amended, of the agencies. Basically statutory law rather than constitutional law governs administrative procedure, although constitutional rights are protected in the administrative process regardless of congressional policy.

The powers Congress delegates to the bureaucracy are extremely important in shaping the impact of administrative adjudication upon the community. For example, the Federal Communications Commission (FCC) has been given the authority to license television and radio stations and determine telephone and telegraph rates in interstate commerce. The *standards* of adjudication set by Congress are simply that the grant of a license must be in the public interest, and rates charged by common carriers, such as American Telephone and Telegraph Company, shall be just and reasonable. The Communications Act of 1934, as amended, seems to give extraordinary power to the FCC, coupled with generally vague standards. Congress really seems to be saying that there is a tremendous job to be done, requiring a great deal of specialized knowledge, and we will simply appoint a commission with the necessary power to do it. What the commission does is at its own discretion. Thus the substantive standards of administrative adjudication are generally within the discretion of the agencies.

The procedures to be followed by the bureaucracy in adjudication are also contained in part in the statutes governing the agencies. In many types of cases the procedures are carefully outlined. Hearings are frequently prescribed, records are required to be kept, and so on. Further, there are often elaborate provisions for judicial review, which suggest that if the agencies step beyond the boundaries of legitimate authority, redress can always be secured in the courts.

Regardless of legal provisions governing administrative procedure and judicial review, the environment of decision making gives the agencies virtually complete discretion. The procedures that are prescribed relate to the formal hearing stage of administrative adjudication, whereas most decisions are made at an informal level.[1] Because of the dominant position of the informal administrative decision making process very few cases, relatively speaking, reach the courts. Individuals and groups use the informal process because it is less time-consuming and expensive, and does not result in straining relations with the agency too much. Further, very little publicity is given to informal proceedings; therefore, many business interests that consider good will an important asset prefer this form of adjudication because the public need never know that they have been involved in illegal or questionable activity of any kind. The same factors that keep private parties away from the formal hearing process result in limiting judicial review. The courts are available, but all too frequently taking a case to them is self-defeating. Moreover, the courts themselves have adopted doctrines of review that give the agencies maximum discretion.

1. See Peter Woll, *Administrative Law: The Informal Process* (Berkeley and Los Angeles: University of California Press, 1963) for an extensive discussion of informal administrative adjudication.

The environment of administrative adjudication is determined directly by the types of cases handled; hence, it varies within and among agencies. Some examples will be illustrative. One of the most powerful and significant agencies with judicial power is the Internal Revenue Service. Elaborate substantive regulations are prescribed by the agency in the Internal Revenue Code relating to corporate and individual income taxes. Because of the complexity of the regulations and a necessary lack of absolute precision in many fields, such as deduction categories, which depend a great deal upon changing circumstances, the Internal Revenue Service has a large amount of discretion in the way it carries out the law. Its interpretation of the law may be challenged formally in the Tax Court or in the judiciary; however, the chances are excellent that these appellate authorities will uphold the Internal Revenue Service. There is a presumption in favor of the agency, and this is well known to those groups and individuals within its jurisdiction. In this respect the Internal Revenue Service is like most administrative agencies.

A second important fact determining the nature of Internal Revenue Service adjudication is that the decision process involves individuals as much as it involves groups. There are at present sixty million individual income tax returns, plus one million corporation returns that must be processed each year, and over twice as much money is collected from individuals as from corporations. Further, the number of cases that must be *adjudicated,* i.e., where there is a case and controversy, is far greater for individuals than for corporations. What effect does this have upon the exercise of judicial power by this agency? It gives the Internal Revenue Service far greater power than would otherwise be the case, because the resources of individuals faced with the problem of challenging an adverse agency decision are proportionately far less than those of corporate groups. Added to the individual's lack of time and money is a fear of the Internal Revenue Service; some people believe they will immediately go to jail for failure to pay their taxes in accordance with the wishes of the agency. For these reasons, the atmosphere is simply not conducive to any kind of an adversary proceeding, and even initial agency decisions go unchallenged as a rule. On the other hand, when corporations are involved, the element of wealth and power enters the adjudicative process. Expensive legal advice is readily available to fight the government all the way to the Supreme Court if necessary, and corporations are able to secure such advice. In administrative law, as in private law, if parties are adversaries, fair adjudication is best achieved when the economic resources of the parties are more or less equal. This is true regardless of the type of procedure employed in adjudication, although it has greater validity in the formal hearing process.

When the Internal Revenue Service decides, after reviewing (auditing) an income tax return that certain claims made by a private party do not conform to regulations, it will inform the individual or group involved that a deficiency exists and that a certain amount is owed to the government. The case and controversy is between the agency on the one hand, and the private party on the other. After a notice of tax deficiency has been made, the agency will attempt to settle the case informally through negotiation with the party concerned. The same type of procedure is employed by other agencies when they make complaints against private parties. Informal procedure saves time and expense, and in this respect benefits the government agency as much as the private party, for, contrary to the views of many observers, the resources of the bureaucracy are limited. Through informal procedure the agencies hope to achieve the greatest amount of enforcement with the least expense. In this area of administrative law over 90 per cent of the cases are settled informally, which is true both for corporations and individuals.

Administrative adjudication may involve cases that are not contested, in the usual sense of that term. For example, if the Internal Revenue Service finds a deficiency in a tax return that the taxpayer does not wish to contest, it can be regarded as an instance of adjudication. This may be difficult to grasp, particularly for those accustomed to thinking of adjudication in terms of traditional court procedure. First, although there may be no contest there may be a case, because the rights and obligations of a particular party are involved. Second, although there may be no contest there is a "controversy" because the agency is challenging the action of an individual or group. The fact that the agency is making a specific determination contrary to the wishes of a private party, and defining the rights and obligations of that party under the law, is sufficient to call the action "adjudication." Administrative adjudication is often uncontested because of factors adverse to the private parties involved, such as expense and the existence of administrative sanctions.

The activities of the Internal Revenue Service illustrate only one area of administrative adjudication, though a very important one. The kinds of cases handled by this agency have been called "complaint cases" because they involve the resolution of a complaint initiated by the government. Complaint cases arise from private activity which is considered a violation of administrative regulations. Complaints may be made to regulatory agencies by private parties, although formal initiation of a complaint is usually made by and in the name of the agency. Individuals or groups often bring possible legal violations to the attention of the relevant agency, which then must decide whether or not this outside complaint is valid and whether proceedings should be initiated against the party in question. The agencies also use their own staffs to investigate business or other private activity within their jurisdiction. If the staff finds something questionable, the agency will be alerted and proceedings may be started to stop the private activity in question. Usually voluntary settlement is secured through informal negotiation, as is illustrated by the Internal Revenue Service process of settling tax cases. Complaint cases fall into the category of adjudication because they relate to specific parties and involve a controversy concerning the extent of legal violation. Further, the agencies have legal authority, given to them by Congress, to render final decisions in this area within narrowly defined limits of judicial review. In actual practice they generally have the power, which is based upon legal authority but goes beyond it, to make final decisions without outside review of any kind.

Examples of complaint cases include: Federal Trade Commission proceedings in alleged cases of deceptive business practice; Civil Aeronautics Board cases involving complaints about airline service; Federal Communications Commission cases concerning complaints against broadcasters and radio operators; Interstate Commerce Commission cases relating to complaints about service, charges, etc., on the part of railroads and truckers; Securities and Exchange Commission cases involving complaints against brokers, and business advisory services; and unfair labor practice cases before the National Labor Relations Board.

Apart from complaint cases, administrative adjudication relates to what may be called "application cases." In many fields individuals and groups wishing to engage in particular types of activity must secure permission from the government agency that regulates their area of interest. They first submit an application presenting their "case" to those having the power of decision. Then, the agency must decide whether or not, and on what condition, it will grant the application. Such an action is adjudication because it involves a specific case and also a "controversy" between the applicant and the agency. If there were no controversy, and all applications were granted automatically, there would be no need for an agency in the first place. In determinations concerning applications, agencies apply very broad standards which usually demand that the "public interest, convenience, and necessity" be served.

Other examples of application cases include: Federal Power Commission, Interstate Commerce Commission, Civil Aeronautics Board, and Federal Communications Commission decisions on license and rate applications; and Securities and Exchange Commission determinations concerning registration statements, the listing of securities, and so on. In all these areas private parties must apply to the relevant agencies for approval of their activities.

Finally, an area of tremendous importance that falls into the application case category is benefit adjudication. Because of the scope and significance of government activity in this field, which will increase in the future, special note should be taken of the two primary agencies involved: the Veterans Administration, and the Bureau of Old-Age and Survivors Insurance within the Department of Health, Education, and Welfare. This area of adjudication is characterized by a large volume of highly technical cases. For example, many involve application of medical criteria to individual cases to determine the nature and extent of physical and mental disabilities. The agencies have been directed not to take an adversary position with respect to applicants. They are to adjudicate in a friendly manner. Nevertheless, this type of decision making is classified as "adjudication" not only because specific parties are involved, but also because the agencies have a great deal of discretion in many case categories in the way they carry out the law. Because benefit laws are highly complex the agencies themselves will usually determine first the kinds of applications that may be submitted, and then decide whether or not the requests for benefits that they initiated themselves will be granted. This may seem rather strange on the surface, but these agencies, like most, are very large and are composed of a variety of specialists that handle different aspects of a case in adjudication.

These case categories indicate that the nature and scope of administrative adjudication differs substantially from court adjudication. The environment of decision making is quite distinct, and the scope of adjudication is as broad as government regulation itself.

Several important aspects of administrative adjudication remain to be discussed. First, the way in which administrative sanctions that derive from the regulatory power of the agencies affect the adjudicative process. Second, problems concerning overlapping jurisdiction of agencies, an area not unlike the judicial analogue. Finally, separate sections will deal with current procedural problems within agencies in adjudication and judicial review.

## ADMINISTRATIVE SANCTIONS AND ADMINISTRATIVE ADJUDICATION

The existence of administrative sanctions is a key distinction between administrative law and other areas of law, particularly in the effect these sanctions have upon the decision making environment of the agencies as opposed to that of the courts. With reference to bureaucracy the term "sanction" includes particular powers possessed by administrative agencies that may be employed against individuals and groups to bring them into line with administrative policy. Sanctions may be specifically stated in statutory law, or they may derive from the general regulatory powers of the agencies. For example, the Federal Communications Act of 1934, governing the operations of the FCC, states that the Commission may revoke a station's license upon finding that the licensee has violated administrative standards. This power of revocation has virtually never been used, because the general regulatory powers of the Commission subsume sanctions that can be highly effective if employed properly. All regulatory statutes contain formal sanctions that may be employed by the administering agencies, but the most effective sanctions usually stem from the fact that important and profitable private activity can not be carried out without the approval of the appropriate agencies; therefore, private parties subject to administrative jurisdiction will not wish to offend the bureaucracy any more than is absolutely necessary, and will in many instances voluntarily acquiesce to agency directives because of *potential* action that might be taken against them.

Extensive regulatory power generates a certain fear of the bureaucracy that frequently makes administrative adjudication unbalanced. An agency may initiate action against a particular group, which will not want to challenge it from fear of future reprisal. The Federal Communications Commission, for example, has no particular power to compel programs of a certain nature to be shown by the television stations throughout the country. It can not say to the CBS, NBC, or ABC networks that this or that program is too violent and can not be used by affiliated stations. When the FCC decides to initiate a complaint against a particular station problems of administrative sanctions enter the picture. In such a situation the station is theoretically faced with the possibility of license revocation, but more practically it is faced with the problem of renewal of its license when its present one expires. In many such cases the FCC succeeds in obtaining its goals from a mere informal inquiry. The possibility of Commission action against station owners causes them to obey the Commission.

The FCC is not the only agency that applies sanctions that profoundly affect the exercise of its judicial functions. In fact, it is one of the weakest in this respect. Station owners and networks can and do ignore the Commission when the Commissioners themselves fail to agree on what action should be taken. The FCC frequently threatens action and dire consequences, but the threat more often than not comes from a minority of the Commissioners. When the Commission is united its sanctions are imposing. In 1961, it ordered a Miami television station off the air and revoked its license, because of misconduct on the part of the owners in securing the license. The misconduct, which consisted of improper political pressure, was also a factor in three other applications for this license that the Commission disqualified from further consideration. The FCC action relating to Channel 10 in Miami came at the end of a long series of public disclosures and attacks concerning the Commission's previous decision in this case; hence, it was unusually severe and designed to prove to critics that the FCC could operate with integrity. At the same time the Commission was taking this drastic action against the owners of Channel 10, its vigorous new chairman, Newton Minow, wanted to hold a public hearing into questionable activity on the part of a New York radio station that was making application for renewal of its license. He was outvoted, along with one other Commissioner, and the renewal was granted without question. Such a public hearing can be by itself an effective sanction against a radio or television station because it publicizes alleged illegal activity; however, in this instance the Commission was too severely split to act.

A notable example of an agency with powerful sanctions is provided by the Securities and Exchange Commission (SEC). This independent regulatory agency has jurisdiction over the stock exchanges and over the investment business generally. Various formal sanctions are written into the statutes that grant the SEC power; however, it rarely employs these formal sanctions. Decision-making by the SEC is almost uniquely affected by the area of its jurisdiction, since the stock markets are by their nature responsive to the behavior and mood of the individual investor. One of the principal jobs of the Commission is to make certain that public information about securities, which includes the kinds of information given the investor by so-called advisers or advisory services, is accurate. The Commission is supposed to protect the public from deceitful practices on the part of those selling or marketing securities. The Securities Act of 1933 requires that companies wishing to sell securities to the public must file with the SEC a registration statement which presents an accurate picture of their financial status. On the basis of this statement a prospectus is issued to potential investors so that they can make up their own minds as to the worth of the securities in question. SEC adjudication involves deciding the basis on which private parties may market securities.

The SEC has potent administrative sanctions because of its ability to delay the marketing of securities, and to publicize anything questionable about the parties involved. The Commission must take positive action to *accelerate* even a normal application that requires very few changes, or amendments. This is because the law requires a twenty-day waiting period after each amendment to a registration statement is made before the issue can be marketed. Unless the Commission agrees to waive this requirement, delay is automatic. This power constitutes an extraordinarily effective sanction; security issues are always hopefully timed to reach the market during a favorable period, and delay results in uncertainty and possible adversity in the stock and bond markets.

Even more important than the Commission's power to delay the issuing of securities is its power to cast a shadow on the reputation of the parties involved by issuing a "stop order," which forbids sale of the securities pending a hearing. Such a hearing automatically raises doubts in financial circles about the soundness of the securities, and does far more harm to a successful sale than Commission delay of the effective registration date. This fact should be remembered and contrasted with the indispensability of hearings in the judicial or common-law decision making model; in this type of administrative activity, hearings that conform to the model virtually preclude a fair judgment because they automatically invoke sanctions adverse to the interests of the private parties.

The net result of the sanctions possessed by the Securities and Exchange Commission is that companies making application for permission to sell their securities will rarely question Commission decisions, which are normally made by the staff, concerning the necessary components of registration statements. The adjudicative process generally prevents the applicant from taking an adversary position; the word of the Commission becomes law. *Formally* a challenge may be made, but practically it is an extremely risky course of action. This is not so much because of the possibility of adverse action by the SEC, but because of unfavorable public reaction. In this respect the sanctions of the SEC differ from those of the Federal Communications Commission.

Administrative sanctions exist because the bureaucracy combines the ability to initiate action with the power to decide particular cases. In other words the problems that arise from sanctions in the exercise of judicial functions by the bureaucracy stem directly from the fact that administrative agencies have regulatory power that combines not only the legislative and judicial powers, but also requires as a result of the combination of these powers that agencies initiate action in the public interest as they define it, and decide cases on the basis of policy standards. In controversies in the courts, parties are placed in adversary positions, and the judge (and sometimes a jury) acts as a third party. In administrative proceedings the "third party" nature of the deciding authorities is frequently absent, because they must function in the interests of broad regulation based upon subjective policy requirements they themselves define. The judicial function becomes a critical part of the enforcement process in the bureaucracy, and cases arise directly as a result of the regulatory power of the administrative branch.

Where sanctions exist they are generally significant only in the sphere of particular agencies. The lack of unity in American bureaucracy generally prevents the possibility of sanctions by one agency from affecting the nature of judicial proceedings before another. A united bureaucracy would present an imposing threat to fair adjudication, which may be illustrated by several incidents that took place during the first years of the Kennedy administration. In 1961 the General Electric and Westinghouse Electric corporations, along with a number of smaller concerns, were convicted for price fixing in a broad range of electrical equipment. Since the case involved a violation of the Sherman Act and the anti-trust laws, it fell within the jurisdiction of the Justice Department to secure the convictions. The executives of these companies were accused of being aware at all times of the flagrantly illegal practices on the part of their subordinates, and some of the executives of both companies were given jail sentences in an unprecedented judicial action in a Federal District Court in Philadelphia. Normally the case would have ended at this point, apart from the damage suits against the companies, and other administrative agencies would have had little if any interest in the situation.

But some months after the General Electric and Westinghouse convictions, the FCC issued a statement to the press which was also sent to the two companies to the effect that the prior activities of their executives in fixing prices for electrical equipment raised serious doubts about the capabilities of the companies to operate the rather large number of television and radio stations they owned. The FCC challenged them to prove that continued operation of their stations would be in the public interest. The companies were told to submit evidence concerning their broadcasting activities, and the Commission indicated that such evidence had to outweigh their record of unlawful conduct.

Although the FCC has some responsibility in the anti-trust field, it was really raising a rather extraneous issue against these large and diversified corporations whose station licenses were up for renewal. It was serving notice that illegal activity under the jurisdiction of outside agencies would be taken into account in its own consideration of whether or not to grant or renew a license, which is of course a judicial decision. In this way the sanctions of the FCC were being used to reinforce those of the Justice Department.

The development of inter-agency cooperation in the anti-trust field was not, in itself, dangerous. Nevertheless, if the practice were to spread to other bureaucratic activities it could in many instances have the effect of inhibiting private individuals and groups from challenging administrative decisions, and hence would distort the decision process in a way that would certainly be considered unfair in terms of the judicial model, and probably in terms of a more flexible model that sought to achieve a fair balance between the rights of the individual and the powers of government.

## PROBLEMS IN OVERLAPPING AGENCY JURISDICTION

It should be noted that lack of cooperation among agencies in the administration of particular laws may result in inconsistent sanctions being employed against private parties. The problem arises when several agencies share jurisdiction, as in the anti-trust field, but disagree on the application of the law. The failure of these agencies to cooperate in their administration of the anti-trust laws produces uncertainty and inaccurate expectations on the part of private companies that may find they have spent a great deal of money and time on a merger proposal they think will be approved by the agency with apparent primary jurisdiction, only to have their activities nullified by another agency.

Confusion in agency jurisdiction has the obvious result of encouraging the large and powerful private interests to play one agency off against another to secure approval for a particular action. This adds a new dimension to the adversary process, bringing in opposition between agencies, alongside opposition between private interests and between private and governmental groups. Lack of cooperation in the bureaucracy is to the advantage of large interests with financial backing, but may be quite detrimental to small groups and individuals with limited resources. The former will play the game to their advantage; the latter will not know where they stand in relation to the agencies that have jurisdiction over them. It is quite possible that one administrative agency will take action against an individual or group that has been acting in accordance with the wishes of another agency, the very reverse of the situation in the General Electric-Westinghouse case. There, adverse sanctions were threatened by the FCC to supplement the action of the Justice Department, because both agencies agreed on the nature of the legal violation the companies had committed.

An interesting example of the confusion that exists because of divided jurisdiction in the administrative process is provided by what will be called the El Paso Natural Gas Co. case (1956–62). The case involved the attempt of El Paso Natural Gas Co. to acquire the Pacific Northwest Pipe Line Corporation. The case was opened in 1956, when El Paso acquired a controlling stock interest in Pacific Northwest, and was ended in 1962, when the Supreme Court, which had been called in to settle the case in 1959, rendered its decision in *California v. Federal Power Commission.*[2] The issues were complex, but essentially the problem to be solved was whether the Federal Power Commission (FPC) had jurisdiction under the Natural Gas Act to make a final de-

2. 369 U.S. 482 (1962).

termination of the validity of the merger, or whether the Justice Department under the Clayton Act had jurisdiction. Many of the problems that arise as a result of overlapping jurisdictions stem from confusing statutory provisions, and this case was no exception. There were good reasons to support either the FPC or the Justice Department on the basis of the relevant statutes. Both had jurisdiction, and it fell to the Supreme Court to make a choice between them in order to resolve the controversy.

The relevant statutory provisions were section 7 of the Clayton Act and section 7 of the Natural Gas Act. The former provides that no company may acquire the *stock* of another if such an acquisition has the effect of substantially lessening competition and creating a monopoly. The Justice Department has the power to enforce the Clayton Act through the courts, along with the Federal Trade Commission and several other independent regulatory agencies (ICC, FCC, CAB, and the Federal Reserve Board), but excluding the Federal Power Commission. From the provisions of the Clayton Act it was clear that the Justice Department had jurisdiction over the El Paso case, because stock acquisition was involved. After El Paso acquired a controlling stock interest in Pacific Northwest, it decided that it wished to merge the *assets* of the two companies. Such a merger of assets had to be approved by the FPC under the terms of section 7 of the Natural Gas Act. Apparently, then, both the Justice Department and the FPC had jurisdiction. The former could legitimately attack the merger as a violation of the Clayton Act, whereas the latter had ultimately to approve the merger of the assets of the two companies, which it could prevent by refusing to issue a certificate of public convenience and necessity.

The sequence of events in the El Paso Natural Gas case indicates that El Paso, which was the direct party in interest, sought to use the Federal Power Commission as a lever against the Justice Department. The Justice Department initially filed suit in the United States District Court in Utah in 1957, seeking to restrain the merger of El Paso and Pacific Northwest through stock acquisition by the former, which it considered to be a violation of section 7 of the Clayton Act. Two weeks after the government action indicating hostility to El Paso's proposed merger, the company filed an application with the FPC for authorization to merge its assets with those of Pacific Northwest in addition to its stock. The company then immediately sought to have the anti-trust action delayed, pending the outcome of its case before the FPC, which it had reason to expect would be favorable. El Paso had acquired a controlling interest in the stock of Pacific Northwest long before its application to the FPC for permission to merge further the assets of the two companies. It is probably not coincidental that its application to the FPC came directly after adverse Justice Department action. The company was attempting to use the divided jurisdiction of these agencies to place the FPC in opposition to the Justice Department.

After application was made to the FPC, infighting began to take place between the FPC and the Justice Department regarding which agency had the power to determine initially whether the merger was valid with respect to the jurisdictional area over which each had control, a merger of assets, and stock acquisition respectively. Any initial decision would substantially shape subsequent action. If the FPC determined that a merger of assets was valid, this would necessarily carry a great deal of weight in opposition to a subsequent anti-trust prosecution in the courts by the Justice Department, and if such a prosecution was carried out the FPC decision would provide substantial evidence for a court decision adverse to the Justice Department. Conversely, prior Justice Department action would prejudice the case before the FPC. The agency, then, which had primary jurisdiction over the case would control in a substantial manner the final decision on the validity of the merger. The FPC gained this initial advantage, and secured a decision from the District Court to which the Justice Department had taken its case to the effect that its decision would await the outcome of the Commission's proceedings.

The FPC approved the merger, and stated that it felt its decision should be immune from further consideration by the Justice Department. The Commission said it had taken section 7 of the Clayton Act into account in its determination of "public convenience and necessity," and found the public interest favored a merger of the two companies. The state of California appealed the FPC's decision to the United States Court of Appeals for the District of Columbia, which affirmed the decision of the Commission. California then appealed to the Supreme Court, which held in *California v. Federal Power Commission* that "orderly procedure" demanded that the Commission should await the decision of the District Court in the original anti-trust suit before rendering its own decision. In other words it decided in favor of initial Justice Department action in combination with the courts. Justice Douglas, for the majority, stated that

> our function is to see that the policy entrusted to the courts is not frustrated by an administrative agency. Where the primary jurisdiction is in the agency, courts withhold action until the agency has acted. The converse should also be true, lest the anti-trust policy whose enforcement Congress in this situation has entrusted to the courts is in practical effect taken over by the Federal Power Commission.[3]

Justice Harlan, speaking for the minority, stated:

> The holding does not turn on any facts or circumstances which may be said to be peculiar to this particular case. It is not limited to Federal Power Commission proceedings. Without adverting to any legal principle or statute to support its decision, the Court appears to lay down a pervasive rule, born solely of its own abstract notions of what "orderly procedure" requires, that seemingly will henceforth govern every agency action involving matters with respect to which the anti-trust laws are applicable and anti-trust litigation is then pending in the courts.
>
> I cannot subscribe to a decision which broadly works such havoc with the proper relationship between the administrative and judicial functions in matters of this kind. The decision . . . in effect transfers to the Anti-trust Division of the Department of Justice regulatory functions entrusted to administrative agencies. . . .[4]

Regardless of Harlan's warning that *California v. Federal Power Commission* would control all subsequent anti-trust proceedings involving divided jurisdiction, the vagueness of statutory standards coupled with agency pursuit of self-interest guaranteed that similar situations would arise in the future.

The criteria applied by the two agencies in their determinations regarding mergers differed. The Justice Department had to determine whether or not a merger would "lessen competition, or . . . tend to create a monopoly"; the Federal Power Commission had to decide whether the proposed merger conformed

3. *Ibid.*, p. 490.
4. *Ibid.*, p. 491.

to the "public convenience and necessity." Although the two standards can easily be interpreted as one and the same thing, this is not likely to be the case where the Justice Department and an independent regulatory agency are concerned. Regulatory agencies tend to become promoters of the industry under their jurisdiction; hence, they are very likely to approve mergers that may improve the economic health of an industry and of particular firms. The Justice Department, on the other hand, has an institutionally oriented attitude opposed to mergers in general because they tend too much to a restraint of trade or monopoly. The regulatory agency tends to have a narrow and protective view; the Justice Department has a broad perspective which leads it to oppose mergers in one industry which would be at the expense of groups outside the industry.

The difference in attitude toward mergers is reinforced by the respective decision processes. The courts are the instruments of adjudication for the Justice Department, whereas a regulatory agency such as the Federal Power Commission has a relatively independent procedure for adjudication that is set forth in its own regulations and in statutory provisions. Procedural patterns in adjudication give the regulatory agencies a great deal of power to shape decisions in terms of their constituencies, which always include as one of the most important components regulated industry groups. Although provision has been made for a certain degree of separation of judicial officers, or hearing examiners, within agencies from the agencies as a whole, they are actually subject to agency control in many respects, with the result that the courts are frequently far more independent in relation to powerful private corporations and groups subject to regulatory jurisdiction, than the respective dependent or independent regulatory agencies. The courts are strongly influenced by direct and substantial interests in adjudication, but not by a *particular* group of interests on a consistent basis.

Because agency attitudes and decision processes tend to favor industry interests, *judicial review* of administrative decisions is frequently initiated by groups that participate only as interested "outside" or "third" parties in administrative proceedings. In some instances they may not participate at all, but will nevertheless challenge an administrative decision because it affects them. For example, rate making decisions directly involve private corporations that wish to gain permission from an agency to charge certain rates to their customers. Their customers may be other corporations or simply the general consumer. The parties most directly concerned with rate making proceedings are usually the companies charging the rate, rather than those paying it. These companies usually spend the greatest amount of time and money in administrative hearings concerning rates, and other items that affect them directly, and favorable decisions are more likely than not obtained. The courts are used as independent appellate bodies by groups that are not able to control the agencies, which frequently results in appeal by third parties. The case of *California v. Federal Power Commission* illustrates this, in that a favorable agency decision for El Paso was appealed by the state of California, which had intervened in the Commission's proceedings because it had an indirect interest in the final decision. It represented the consumers of California, who presumably might have something to gain by preventing a merger that could result in a restraint of trade.

## Administrative Law, the Constitution, and the Common Law

The Constitution poses several problems to the existence of administrative power of a judicial nature. Within the concept of separation of powers there is no provision for the exercise of judicial power outside the judiciary. But judicial power was given to the agencies because it forms an essential part of effective *regulatory power*. Further, there were deficiencies in the courts which made them ineffective for the purpose of securing strong government regulation of industry. In any event the judicial power that now resides in the bureaucracy is not there to enable it to check the judiciary, which would have to be the reason in terms of constitutional theory.

The existence of judicial power in the hands of administrative agencies is not really incidental to the executive power as it is generally defined, and particularly not as it was defined in the Constitution. It is incidental to regulatory power, which is far broader than the executive function, and encompasses all three primary powers of government.

## THE ROLE OF THE COURTS UNDER THE CONSTITUTION

Article III of the Constitution states that "the judicial power of the United States shall be vested in one Supreme Court, and in such inferior courts as the Congress may from time to time ordain and establish." The courts were to be independent of the other two branches of government because the nature of judicial power demands it. We have indicated that American constitutional theory requires that one branch should not exercise to a significant degree the powers of coordinate branches, and in particular that the executive should not have substantial legislative and judicial power. This theory was clarified in greater detail by Hamilton in *Federalist* 78.

First, Hamilton noted that in terms of organization "the complete independence of the courts of justice is peculiarly essential in a limited Constitution." This is important initially because the judiciary, possessing the power of *judicial review*, must act as a check upon the legislative body and upon its general power to make laws. The Constitution does not intend, according to Hamilton, that the legislators shall have the ability "to substitute their *will* to that of their constituents. It is far more rational to suppose, that the courts were designed to be an intermediate body between the people and the legislature, in order, among other things, to keep the latter within the limits assigned to their authority. The interpretation of the laws is the proper and peculiar province of the courts."

Further, Hamilton stated that judicial independence is necessary "to guard the Constitution and the rights of individuals from the effects of those ill humors, which the arts of designing men, or the influence of particular conjunctures, sometimes disseminate among the people themselves, and which, though they speedily give place to better information, and more deliberate reflection, have a tendency, in the meantime, to occasion dangerous innovations in the government, and serious oppressions of the minor party in the community." That is, the judges are supposed to protect the people from themselves, a job they could not perform properly if they were dependent upon the people directly, or indirectly, by being responsible to the legislature.

Finally, judicial independence exists to protect the rights of individuals generally in the adjudication of cases. Congress initially determines the jurisdiction of the courts and, hence, the type of cases that will come before the judiciary. But an independent judge can do a lot to shape the way in which the law is implemented. The judges determine the real nature of the law and the protections that will be afforded individuals, regardless of what Congress does.

The courts are competent to judge issues involving the Constitution and individual rights not only because their independence makes them less subject to political whims and passions, but also as a direct result of permanent tenure during good behavior, which will permit judicial specialization.

The right of the courts to exercise the power of judicial review was firmly established by Marshall in *Marbury v. Madison* (1803), in which he stated: "It is emphatically the province and duty of the judicial department to say what the law is. Those who apply the rule to particular cases, must of necessity expound and interpret that rule. If two laws conflict with each other, the courts must decide on the operation of each." [5]

## THE CONSTITUTIONAL BASIS OF ADMINISTRATIVE LAW

The development of the bureaucracy has forced the courts to be extremely imaginative and flexible in the creation of doctrines that permit administrative agencies judicial power. This has been equally true with respect to administrative legislation as we will see in the next chapter. The constitutional question presented by bureaucratic exercise of judicial functions is how to reconcile them with the provision in Article III requiring that judicial power reside in the Supreme Court and inferior courts to be established by Congress.

The first justification for the location of judicial power in the hands of the bureaucracy is that the Constitution gives *Congress* the power to create the entire judicial system with the exception of the Supreme Court. Congress determines how many courts

5. 1 Cranch 137, 177 (1803).

there will be, the number of judges, the jurisdiction of the courts, and so forth. The only thing it cannot touch is the Supreme Court and its *original jurisdiction;* Congress can change by law the appellate jurisdiction of the Supreme Court, as well as the number of judges on the Court. If it does not like something the Court is doing it can simply cut off jurisdiction from the type of case in which objectionable decisions are being rendered, provided the cases do not fall within the original jurisdiction of the Court. The latter includes only cases involving ambassadors, and disputes among states or in which the state is a party. This part of the Court's jurisdiction is extremely narrow. Virtually all of the important cases arise in the area of appellate jurisdiction; thus the potential power of Congress over the Supreme Court is very great indeed.

As far as the subordinate judicial system is concerned Congress determines everything. For this reason it has been possible from a constitutional viewpoint for Congress to place judicial power wherever it wishes. It has the power to set up administrative agencies and give them judicial power. It determines the kinds of appeals that may be taken to the courts from administrative decisions. It may say, as it has with respect to actions of the Veterans Administration, that administrative decisions shall be final and conclusive on all questions of law and fact. This virtually precludes judicial interference. Using this constitutional power Congress has delegated judicial power to the bureaucracy.

The courts have no desire to usurp the powers of coordinate branches of the government, and they have a deep respect for their role in the constitutional system. As a result, when Congress wishes to delegate particular powers to the administrative branch the courts will generally not raise objections. But while the judiciary has acquiesced in congressional delegation of judicial power to the bureaucracy, it has had to find constitutional justifications for permitting this apparent incursion on the courts' domain. One might say that the courts have had to find a way to rationalize in constitutional terms administrative power of a judicial nature. They have done this in a rather ingenious way. Essentially, they have stated that there are two kinds of judicial power: judicial power, stemming from Article III, and judicial power that does not stem from Article III. The former is that which is normally considered appropriate for courts, and the latter involves power judicial in nature but not clearly provided for in Article III. By making this distinction every problem concerning the proper location of judicial power becomes a matter of definition. The Constitution says only that the powers that fall under the heading of Article III must reside in courts (that is, constitutional courts), and outside of the original jurisdiction of the Supreme Court Congress itself determines which powers are bestowed by Article III and which are not.

The courts, then, have found no constitutional objection to congressional placement of judicial power in the hands of administrative agencies. They have even aided the delegation of such power by inventing the necessary constitutional rationalizations. To some extent the courts must function in line with the political expectations of the community, which are more directly reflected in the other branches of the government. The reasons for establishing an administrative process with effective regulatory power, and hence effective judicial power, were compelling from the political and economic standpoint. The courts themselves had sabotaged numerous congressional attempts at regulation which used them as the judicial arms of regulatory systems. It would have been impossible politically, and questionable constitutionally, for the judiciary to declare unconstitutional congressional establishment of regulatory and other administrative agencies with judicial power. This fact does not in any way lessen the serious constitutional implications of the extraordinary power of the bureaucracy in the judicial realm. One of the principal ideas behind placing judicial power in a separate court system was to limit the other branches of government, and in particular the law-making power. When legislative and judicial power are combined in the same hands this important constitutional check is not present.

## ADMINISTRATIVE LAW AND THE COMMON LAW

The problems presented to the American constitutional system by the development of administrative law are not nearly as difficult to resolve as those that arise from the conflict between administrative law and the *common law*. The Anglo-American legal system is based upon common-law concepts and practices, and the Constitution can properly be termed a common-law constitution.[6] The term "common law" refers to legal principles and practices, made by judges, that have characterized the Anglo-American legal system. Of course these principles have changed from one period to another, but in the last few centuries some fairly consistent ideas have emerged that express the fundamental basis of the common-law system.

Rooted in common law is the principle that matters of a clearly judicial nature must be decided in courts that are properly organized and staffed with judges. This is because judges are knowledgeable not only in the substance of the law, as Hamilton pointed out, but in the process of reasoning from fact to conclusion. Courts by their very nature must be independent. Once the judiciary becomes dependent upon the executive or legislative branches it will cease to be part of a true common-law system.

Much of the philosophy of the common law was stated by Sir Edward Coke in the seventeenth century, in order to justify the position the courts of common law were taking against James I. This was a struggle on the part of the judiciary for supremacy in its own field. James wanted the courts to be subject to his direction as far as his royal prerogative was involved in particular cases, but Coke felt that only he, as Chief Justice, and those trained in the law could properly interpret the common law. Interference by the executive could not be tolerated. The common law, broadly conceived, encompassed the entire governmental system and allocated powers and rights to branches of the government and to private citizens. The common law, then, included the constitution and large areas of substantive law. By defining the common law in such broad terms Coke was really calling for a dominant judicial department that would be the ultimate arbiter of all constitutional and legal questions. The role of the courts in this ideal common-law system would have been far more significant

6. For excellent discussions of the common-law basis of the Constitution see Edward S. Corwin, *The "Higher Law" Background of American Constitutional Law* (Ithaca: Cornell University Press, 1955); and J. A. C. Grant, *Our Common Law Constitution* (Boston: Boston University Press, 1960). For a broad and definitive analysis of American political thought in the 17th and 18th centuries see Clinton Rossiter, *Seedtime of the Republic* (New York: Harcourt, Brace, 1953).

than their intended role under the American Constitution. The judiciary was to be the most powerful branch of government, and was to have a far more positive role than that of merely acting as a check upon coordinate branches. In the American system the judiciary interprets a written constitution, but in a common-law system the courts apply general rules of reason, which may or may not derive from written documents, to prevent arbitrary action from any source, governmental or nongovernmental, in the community.

Consider the following two passages from Coke's writings. In rendering a decision in one famous case he pointed out that "it appears in our books, that in many cases, the common law will control acts of Parliament, and sometimes adjudge them to be utterly void: for when an act of Parliament is against common right and reason, or repugnant, or impossible to be performed, the common law will control it, and adjudge such act to be void." [7] The power of the judiciary was not only to extend to Parliament, but was to have general application. In speaking of the jurisdiction of the Court of Kings Bench he noted:

. . . this court hath not only jurisdiction to correct errors in judicial proceeding, but other errors and misdemeanors extrajudicial tending to the breach of the peace, or oppression of the subjects, or raising of faction, controversy, debate, or any other manner of misgovernment; so that no wrong or injury, either public or private, can be done, but that this shall be reformed or punished in one court or other by due course of law.[8]

This suggests that the power of the courts was to be pervasive. They were to make law as well as apply it.

The maintenance of a dominant judiciary acting on the basis of common-law principles came to be identified in much legal theory as equivalent to the supremacy of law. One of the basic premises of common-law theory was that the *executive* would tend to encroach more on the judicial field than the legislature, although in some instances collusion might exist between the legislature and the executive for this purpose. Coke's writings extolling the virtues of judicial supremacy were directed almost

7. *Dr. Bonham's Case,* 8 Co. 118a (1610), 77 English Reports 652.
8. 4 Institutes 71.

entirely against the King, who was understandably considered the gravest threat to the maintenance of an independent and powerful judicial branch. Throughout history it is the executive that has been considered by legal theorists to be the principal opponent to the maintenance of the common-law system. In the seventeenth century this idea was expressed by complete opposition to any kind of executive control of the judiciary; in the nineteenth century it was considered of crucial importance that "officials," i.e., those employed by the executive branch, be subject to common-law jurisdiction; in the twentieth century, the development of administrative law caused a variety of responses from common-law theorists that will be analyzed below. The fear of executive encroachment on the common-law system contrasts sharply with one of the basic premises of American constitutional thought, namely, that it is the legislative branch that will present the gravest threat to coordinate branches.

In the nineteenth century the best expression of common-law theory is to be found in Dicey's historic *Introduction to the Study of the Law of the Constitution* (1885),[9] which exerted a profound and prolonged effect upon British legal thought, and indirectly upon legal theory in the United States. It is not possible here to go deeply into the complexities of Dicey's thought, but the context of administrative law can not be understood without examining the essence of his famous treatise. Dicey was expressing what he felt was the true nature of the common-law system as it had evolved in Great Britain. Central to this system was the presence of the rule of law, which resulted from three characteristics of the common law.

First, "no man is punishable or can be lawfully made to suffer in body or goods [life, liberty, or property] except for a distinct breach of law established in the ordinary legal manner before the *ordinary courts of the land.* In this sense the rule of law is contrasted with every system of government based on the exercise by persons in authority of wide, arbitrary, or discretionary powers of constraint." [10] In this system the "ordinary courts" are the common-law courts, and the "ordinary legal manner" is equivalent

9. A. V. Dicey, *Introduction to the Study of the Law of the Constitution* (London: Macmillan, 1885).
10. Dicey, *op. cit.* note 9 (8th ed., 1915), pp. 183–184. Italics added.

to common-law procedure, which by that time had become precisely defined. Essentially, this procedure involved proper hearing and possible appeal before judgment could be rendered.

Second, the rule of law means "not only that . . . no man is above the law, but (what is a different thing) that . . . *every man, whatever be his rank or condition,* is subject to the ordinary law of the realm and amenable to the jurisdiction of the ordinary tribunals." [11] Here Dicey is referring to the fact that public officials are not immune from judicial scrutiny if they violate the common law.

Finally, Dicey points out that in the common law "the general principles of the constitution (as for example the right to personal liberty . . .) are with us the result of judicial decisions determining the rights of private persons in particular cases brought before the courts; whereas under many foreign constitutions the security (such as it is) given to the rights of individuals results, or appears to result, from the general principles of the constitution." [12] In brief, "our constitution . . . is a judge-made constitution, and it bears on its face all the features, good or bad, of judge-made law." [13]

Dicey echoes Coke in his elevation of the judiciary to the pinnacle of the constitutional system. Also, Dicey, like Coke, was more concerned with executive encroachment on the judiciary than with the possible expansion of the legislature in this direction. Coke was reacting against the King's attempts to control the judiciary for his own purposes, and Dicey was reacting against the French system of administrative law (*droit administratif*) and against the development of administrative law in Great Britain. At the beginning of the twentieth century he reluctantly admitted that there was increasing evidence that administrative agencies were beginning to assume judicial functions, and that because of this the rule of law as he defined it was being placed in jeopardy. Although Coke may have won his victory and established judicial supremacy in the common-law system, the doctrine of the rule of law at the time of Dicey was to face the

11. *Ibid.,* p. 189.
12. *Ibid.,* p. 191.
13. *Ibid.,* p. 192.

more formidable obstacle of a combination of an expanding bureaucracy with judicial power. The battle was to be joined, but the bureaucracy was to win.

## AMERICAN CONSTITUTIONAL LAW AND THE COMMON LAW CONTRASTED

Although the American Constitution is basically a common-law document, it does not elevate the judicial branch to the extent that Dicey and his adherents would have favored. There have been many American common-law theorists, like Roscoe Pound, who lament the lessening power of the judiciary over the bureaucracy and feel that it has resulted in a subversion of the common-law system.[14] However, the allocation of powers in our Constitution makes it very easy to bypass the judiciary in the allotment of judicial functions as has been noted previously. American constitutional theory does not place unusual power in the hands of the courts. It is true that Hamilton, who was more in favor of a strong judiciary than many at that time, had a fairly broad conception of judicial review and its importance to the maintenance of the constitutional system. He recognized that at numerous points the judiciary could prevent the implementation of arbitrary action by Congress. At the same time he stressed that the judiciary would have to be checked, and judicial review was to be primarily for the purpose of keeping the actions of the other branches within well defined constitutional boundaries. It was not to enable the courts to substitute their will for that of the people, or for the specific provisions of the Constitution. The law was not to be judge-made, it was to emanate from the people as expressed in the Constitution. The courts were to be under the Constitution as much as any other branch.

## THE NATURE OF COMMON-LAW PROCEDURE

Exactly *why* under the common law is it imperative that the judiciary monopolize judicial functions? Common-law theorists

14. Roscoe Pound, *The Spirit of the Common Law* (Boston: Marshall Jones Co., 1921).

justify total court supervision of the judicial function on the grounds that the basic purpose of adjudication—protection of the rights of the *individual* through the *accurate determination of the facts* of the particular case—is best fulfilled by the personnel, structure, and procedure of the courts. Not only are judges expert in substantive law and independent, but common-law procedure, which the judiciary follows in many types of cases, is designed specifically to assure the protection of individual interests.

What are the fundamental attributes of common-law procedure? First, the party or parties charged with a particular offense, or involved generally in a case and controversy, must be given sufficient notice of the nature of their offense in time to prepare their case. Like all areas of legal procedure this is a highly complex matter. It is not easy to define what constitutes proper notice in a given set of circumstances, although there are judicial rules that may be applied. Second, once notice has been served, the parties must ideally be given the opportunity to present their case in an open hearing before a judge (and sometimes a jury), who will render a decision on the basis of the record developed by the parties themselves. This part of the process is for the purpose of determining relevant facts concerning the parties. The hearing procedure therefore is structured to exclude irrelevant testimony, and to gain maximum information from the parties through cross-examination, and so forth. It is of the utmost significance that the information upon which the decision is to be made is to be gained from the parties through questioning by the parties. In other words the record is made entirely by the parties themselves on the basis of the information they possess, which means that the decision reflects the individual interests represented directly in the hearing. Finally, after the process has been exhausted, an opportunity for appeal should be present within legally prescribed limits. The entire case can not be reheard except under highly unusual circumstances; however, particular points in question, for example, whether adequate evidence has been introduced to support conclusions reached, may be subject to review by a higher court.

# The Transfer of Judicial Power to Administrative Agencies

To some extent administrative exercise of judicial power is accidental. It was not until the first decade of the twentieth century that administrative power was generally recognized to include judicial functions, and it was not until the New Deal that the American Bar Association and other legal groups began to emphasize that administrative agencies were exerting virtually a revolutionary effect upon our legal system.

How would our system of government work if the courts retained control over judicial functions? This can readily be illustrated by a few examples from history. In order to retain judicial supremacy in the common-law sense, and to a lesser degree in terms of the American constitutional system of separation of powers, the courts would have the responsibility of hearing in the first instance all cases and controversies under statutory and constitutional law. It would mean that administrative agencies would act as prosecuting arms of the government when they functioned in the judicial area. The final decision-making power would reside in the judiciary, and the agencies would have to plead their cases before the judges. Judicial procedure would be employed for all case disposition, with the resulting emphasis upon individual interests.

In the past the courts have exercised not only all judicial functions, but also what in modern terminology would be called administrative functions. For example, during the American colonial period and part of the nineteenth century the courts acted as rate-making bodies, setting tolls for public roads, and so on. They possessed various kinds of regulatory power, and in terms of the common law they were the correct repository of such power. In many instances the courts developed general rules through case by case determinations that became in effect legislation. In the absence of interest by legislative bodies it was only natural that the courts should step in to establish such rules. The courts thus resembled modern administrative agencies, possessing almost unchecked legislative and judicial power. For example, before statutory standards were created, there were all sorts of common-law rules governing how an employee could receive compensation for an injury resulting from his employment. The common law was substantive as well as procedural in nature, and in both respects it was shaped entirely by judicial action.

At the present, anti-trust litigation provides a good example of a field in which primary jurisdiction resides in the courts. The Justice Department must rely entirely on the judiciary for enforcement. Many other agencies engaged in anti-trust enforcement have varying degrees of power independent of the courts, most notably the Federal Trade Commission; but even the FTC shares powers with the judiciary to some extent. The Justice Department acts as the primary prosecuting body, bringing many cases to the courts. It can not act independently to prevent restraints of trade because Congress has been unwilling to give it this power, ever since it passed the Sherman Act in 1890. Once again it is important to point out that the extent of judicial power over administrative agencies is determined by Congress, except as constitutional issues may be involved; in that case the courts will take jurisdiction regardless of congressional intent to the contrary.

Although agencies such as the Justice Department must rely upon judicial enforcement of their policies in particular cases, in relative terms the power of the judiciary to control administrative action by exercising primary jurisdiction in administrative law has virtually vanished. The Justice Department is the exception rather than the rule.

## DEFICIENCIES IN THE JUDICIAL SYSTEM

The courts were unable to meet the demands that were made for the establishment of regulatory agencies; hence they were displaced in both the substantive and procedural areas. Their powers to determine substantive law were taken away in many regulatory fields as were their powers of implementation. In part, the courts failed to meet modern regulatory needs because of cumbersome *procedure*. More significant was the failure of common law to meet *substantive* requirements that arose primarily from an increase in democratic demands upon government.

## THE COMMON LAW AS SUBSTANTIVE LAW

Picture for a moment government and society in the nineteenth century. *Laissez faire* was the operative ideal for much of the period, although the government acted as a promoter of business in many areas through tariffs, railroad subsidies, and so forth. But in general the sphere of legislative action was limited in comparison with what was to come in the twentieth century. The limitation of *statutory* law resulted directly in an increase in the scope of judge-made *common law*. Provided legislatures did not act the courts were frequently free to formulate all kinds of doctrines governing labor and business. The lack of legislative action meant that there was no particular conflict between the courts and Congress or state legislative bodies. Why was Congress relatively inactive? Because demands for action, particularly in regulatory fields, were rare until the last part of this period.

The legislation shaped by judicial action in the nineteenth century reflected a bias that stemmed from the position and procedure of the courts. They were largely independent; hence, they did not have to respond to pressure by the general public as did Congress and the President. This does not mean, of course, that judges do not accept the principles of constitutional democracy prevalent in the American community. But the courts were originally, and in general still are, purposely placed outside the direct democratic process. This fact made it possible and probable that judicial decisions would be somewhat out of touch with the more direct demands that were being placed upon Congress and the President from various groups in the community. Judicial procedure gave an advantage to groups and individuals more wealthy than the norm, for litigation is a time-consuming and expensive process. The judges themselves were rather conservative. They tended to be wealthy and somewhat detached from the people, in sharp contrast with the politicians, whose success depended then as now upon maintaining close contact with the needs and aspirations of the people. It is not entirely inaccurate to characterize the Supreme Court during the latter decades of the nineteenth century as the "property court," a term frequently used. The emphasis of this Court, as well as that of the judiciary generally, was upon the protection of private property, which was only natural, given the environment of judicial decision making. Even in the face of congressional opposition judicial protection of private property did not finally break down until the late 1930s, when the Supreme Court agreed that in some areas a more general public interest takes precedence over demands from wealthy private property interests.

When Congress and state legislative bodies began responding to demands for regulation in the late nineteenth century it was inevitable that the substantive standards developed would be in conflict with the common law; this, in fact, was one of the reasons for new legislation in the first place. The common law was considered inadequate to meet the complex problems arising from rapid industrial growth. At least it did not reflect the political demands of the time. The legal relationships established by the common law were not wanted by the newly powerful political groups; hence, an appeal was made to Congress and other legislative bodies to change the *substantive* legal rules that prevailed by substituting new standards for judicial legislation. The requirements of regulation were not met by the common-law judiciary in the substantive sense, nor in the procedural realm.

Those who have the power to implement the law through judicial determinations have in effect the power to control exactly what criteria will be used. Because the common-law courts were unwilling to change the substantive criteria of the law, the only way legislative bodies could assure the implementation of new and different standards was to create new agencies for enforcement; hence, the administrative agency became a common device to circumvent the courts and the substantive standards they insisted upon.

## DEFICIENCIES IN JUDICIAL PROCEDURE

Apart from the problems presented by judicial insistence upon the maintenance of substantive policy standards that conflicted with those of legislative bodies at all governmental levels, judicial supremacy involved difficulties because of the nature of judicial *procedure*. In effect, this procedure is not suited to achieve the goals of effective and fair government regulation, in terms of the political demands that are placed upon government. In order to realize these goals, administrative procedure frequently emphasizes requirements of speed, lack of expense, and *expertise* in the area involved. Judicial procedure is somewhat inflexible in its emphasis upon notice and hearings as indispensable components of the decision making process, which may be entirely appropriate in some instances, but highly inappropriate in others. The record for decision in administrative law must contain more than the facts and opinions of the immediate and direct interests involved in a particular case. It is doubtful in many cases that judicial procedures, such as cross-examination, will bring out the necessary facts and their relation to broader policy considerations. Judicial procedure thus tends to shape the characteristics of substantive law, making it a reflection of direct and substantial interests. In administrative law the same result has been achieved in those agencies where primary emphasis has been placed upon the necessity of adhering to the judicial decision making model.

The element of time is always important to the realization of a just decision in a particular case and controversy. Under judicial procedure a case may stretch out over a long period, occasioning severe hardship for one or both parties involved. If administrative procedure imitates full-fledged court procedure several or more years may pass before a decision is made. On the other hand, if informal procedure is employed decisions can be made very rapidly.

The problem of time in the administrative process may be illustrated by reference to the Federal Power Commission. This independent regulatory agency has to pass on many classifications of rates charged to the consumer by natural gas companies. For the purpose of illustration a rate case can be considered as an instance of administrative adjudication. The FPC must determine in a particular case, with reference to a limited number of specified parties, the validity of the rates they wish to charge the public. Such validation involves, in effect, a controversy between private interests and the agency.

The FPC has attempted to dispose of rate cases and other related cases through a hearing process, which it feels is mandatory because of statutory requirements. The fact is, however, that it can not possibly dispose through hearings of all the cases relating to the natural gas industry over which it has jurisdiction. As a general rule, it permits a rate increase to go into effect upon application by a private company; after a hearing has been held on the validity of such an increase any reduction in the rate will be refundable to the consumers affected on a retroactive basis. At the present pace it will take the FPC ten or twenty years to determine whether or not present charges to consumers for natural gas are in fact valid; thus, in 1980 it may decide that a rate charged in 1960 was not proper and require the company involved to refund the overcharge to the consumers affected, few of whom will be around to receive their checks because they will have moved, died, or will be otherwise unavailable. In areas in which Commission authorization is required before companies can engage in certain kinds of activity, delay may mean considerable hardship to the parties involved and may have a profound economic effect. For example, before many companies will embark upon a program of expansion they may want to know what rates they can charge for the particular service they will give. If they want to construct new facilities, FPC delay would affect a wide range of companies involved.

What is the answer for the FPC? It must find a way to expedite its procedure: the judicial decision making model, although to some extent altered by the Commission, is not the solution. The problems faced by the FPC and other agencies that rely heavily on judicial procedure would be even greater if left to the courts. The courts simply could not handle the volume of cases that arise under regulatory statutes and that fall within the jurisdiction of administrative agencies. It is quite common for one agency, like the Internal Revenue Service, Veterans Administration, or the Social Security Administration, to handle more cases in a year than the entire federal court system combined. The figure for the federal courts is under two hundred thousand cases a year; the Internal Revenue Service handles close to a million; the Veterans Administration around two million.

Finally, one of the most notable difficulties presented by judicial procedure in relation to political demands for regulation is that the courts can not initiate action. The courts are umpires; they are passive. Administrative agencies, as agents of congressional policy are not supposed to be umpires. They reflect group demands for positive action. They are active, and initiate action in accordance with their policy interests. For example, when the Federal Trade Commission ferrets out deceptive practices, either through its own investigations or through information gained from an outside source, it initiates action in the name of the FTC against the party involved. It then adjudicates the very case it initiates. If the case reaches a formal hearing and goes to a hearing examiner for initial decision, it is not at that point subject to Commission control. But after the examiner renders his decision, the Commission may reverse it. The result is that the FTC actually controls the kinds of decisions rendered in most of the cases it initiates. Many administrative agencies, like the FTC, initiate action in what they consider to be the public interest. Their control of the judicial function means that they can complete the action they begin, rather than making it possible for an outside group to veto their decisions.

## JUDICIAL VS. ADMINISTRATIVE PERSONNEL

An argument can be made that the judge is less suited to the tasks of modern administration than his counterpart in the bureaucracy, which is the old argument about the generalist versus the expert. Administrative decisions that are judicial in nature need to be made by individuals who have had the opportunity to specialize in the subject matter: this is called institutional decision making. Thus the staff of an administrative agency will be composed of specialists such as lawyers, economists, and engineers, all of whom may be important in decision-making. The administrative agency can use more individuals in the decision process who have had an opportunity to specialize in an area which relates their special competence to a specific regulatory field. The judge, normally, has been trained as a lawyer. Usually he must hear cases in a variety of areas that encompass a very wide spectrum. He will jump from divorce law to criminal law to estate law, etc. His task is truly an imposing one. If in addition to the very wide competence expected of him, the judge were suddenly required to master the problems of administrative regulation as well as other areas involving administrative adjudication, his task would be impossible. A division of labor has characterized industrial society, and the need for such a division justifies by itself the exercise of judicial functions beyond the realm of the court system.

## Administrative Law and Internal Agency Procedure

The scope and significance of administrative adjudication raise many problems concerning the way the judicial function should be exercised in the American system of government. The constitutional and common-law context within which judicial power is supposed to function has been noted. It is now necessary to consider some of the more important attempts that have been made to fit administrative adjudication into this framework.

The extensive delegation of judicial functions to administrative agencies was the direct result of the need to bypass both the substantive and procedural policies of the courts. Agencies were supposed to be flexible in both areas to meet regulatory requirements. At first, those groups within the American Bar Association that were later to become concerned with the growing power of the bureaucracy in the judicial area more or less ignored the development of the agencies. Some theorists, like Roscoe Pound, sounded an alarm in the early part of the twentieth century, stating that "executive justice" was beginning to replace "justice according to law," that is, the common law. Pound equated administrative procedure to Star Chamber proceedings, and noted that a vast change would have to take place in both the substantive and procedural aspects of the common law if the increasing power of the agencies was to be curbed. In 1914, in the *Columbia Law Review*, he wrote:

The experience of the past indicates that if we improve the output of judicial justice till the adjustment of human relations by our courts is brought into better accord with the moral sense of the public at large and is achieved without unreasonable, not to say prohibitive, delay and expense, the onward march of executive justice will soon cease. But we [the legal profession] must be vigilant. Legislatures are pouring out an ever-increasing volume of laws. The old judicial machinery has been found inadequate to enforce them. They touch the most vital interests of the community, and it demands enforcement. Hence the executive is turned to. Summary administrative action becomes the fashion. An elective judiciary, sensitive to the public will, yields up its prerogatives, and the return to a government of man is achieved. If we are to be spared a season of oriental justice, if we are to preserve the common-law doctrine of supremacy of law, the profession and the courts must take up vigorously and fearlessly the problem of today—how to *administer* the law to meet the demands of the world that is.[15]

This expresses perfectly the contempt felt by conservative common-law theorists for administrative adjudication. To them, of course, the only solution was to transfer all judicial functions to the courts.

It soon became evident, however, that administrative agencies were to be a permanent fixture in the government. Men like Pound recognized by the time the New Deal had arrived that the old common-law dream of judicial supremacy could not be achieved. It was then obviously necessary, they felt, to do two things. First, make the agencies themselves as much like courts as possible when they exercise judicial functions. Second, expand judicial review as much as possible. At the beginning of the New Deal, in what was a delayed recognition that administrative law could not be abolished, the American Bar Association turned its attention to reforming the administrative process in accordance with these objectives.

The American Bar Association appointed its first committee on administrative law in 1933, and its first report echoed the concerns of men like Pound in its statement that:

When . . . the administrative official exercises a quasi-judicial function, he may be expected to conform to the sort of procedure which has been found best adapted to the determination of the rights and obligations of the individual in his controversies with other individuals and with the government. Certain fundamental safeguards of notice, opportunity for hearing, and determination or review of issues of fact and of law by an independent tribunal (and eventually, on questions of law at least, by a court) are involved, and, indeed, are necessary if justice is to be done to the individual.[16]

15. Roscoe Pound, "Justice According to Law," 14 *Columbia Law Review* 1, at 21–22 (1914).
16. "Report of the Special Committee on Administrative Law," 58 *American Bar Association Reports* 407, at 410 (1933).

The emphasis during this early period of legal concern with the administrative process was upon the *procedural* rather than the substantive aspects of administrative law. Of course many of the more conservative elements in the American Bar Association were basically opposed to the kind of governmental expansion that was taking place under the New Deal, and their answer was to try to place the agencies within a rigid set of controls. Other groups within the Bar Association, however, recognized the necessity of regulatory agencies but felt a genuine concern that the judicial procedures of the bureaucracy conform to those of the courts, with the courts exercising judicial review as a last resort.

The Association put on an intensive drive during the New Deal period to secure the passage of a general statute designed to mold the procedure of all agencies engaged in adjudication and rule making in the image of the courts. Such a general statute would contrast sharply with what had been the common practice of shaping the procedure of each agency in its enabling statute in terms of the particular job it was supposed to do. In 1940, Congress, in response to American Bar Association pressures, passed the Walter-Logan bill which was an extreme attempt to control administrative procedure, only to have it vetoed by President Roosevelt. The veto was not overridden. This Act essentially would have compelled administrative agencies to hold hearings similar to those held by courts in all cases of adjudication and rule making. It would have meant an extraordinary change in administrative practice and would have imposed an impossible burden upon the agencies. The Act did not take into account the vital role played by informal procedure in administrative adjudication, and its requirements for hearings in the legislative area of rule making did not conform to either constitutional or common-law theory. In addition, the Walter-Logan bill provided for judicial review of virtually all administrative decisions of a judicial nature; thus, it ignored the careful distinction the judiciary had been developing with respect to review of administrative decisions between points of law and points of fact. The former were completely reviewable, the latter only as they related to points of law.

World War II interrupted any serious consideration of a general statute to control administrative procedure, but in 1946 the

American Bar Association finally achieved some of its objectives when the Administrative Procedure Act became law.[17] This Act attempted to establish more uniform hearing procedures among the agencies. It provided for greater independence for those administrators, called hearing examiners, who conduct initial administrative proceedings that are adjudicative in nature. It also required that the agencies give more publicity to their regulations than in the past. Finally, it expanded the scope of judicial review.

Because the Administrative Procedure Act (APA) is the only general statute governing agency procedure in adjudication and rule making today its provisions should be noted briefly. First, where there is a previous statutory requirement for hearings before decisions can be rendered in particular types of cases, the APA specifies that such hearings are to be conducted in accordance with certain judicial standards. Since such requirements are relatively rare, the standards of the APA have limited applicability. For example, when an agency such as the Federal Communications Commission renders decisions in many case categories under its jurisdiction it is not compelled by the particular statutes governing it to hold hearings; thus, the APA does not become operative. When, on the other hand, its own statutes require hearings, the procedural standards the agency would have to follow are those contained in the APA. In this way the exigencies of the administrative process are taken into account, and variations in procedure among different agencies are recognized as valid. Finally, it should be noted that where there is a statutory requirement for a hearing it generally means in effect, even if it is not so stated, that only an opportunity for a hearing will be provided; thus, for the many reasons noted previously, the parties involved may wish to settle informally, which nullifies any provisions governing the nature of the hearing procedure.

What are the judicial standards that the Administrative Procedure Act makes applicable to hearings that are required by non-APA statutory provisions? Generally, in the area of formal administrative proceedings the APA requires procedures analogous in many respects to the judicial or common-law model, although never as strict as those decision processes. Thus, notice must be given of formal administrative proceedings; a separation

17. 60 Stat. 237 (1946), 5 U.S.C. Nos. 1001–1011.

of prosecuting and adjudicative functions within the same agency is to be maintained; certain rules of evidence are to prevail; a record of the proceedings is to be kept; the hearing examiner is to make an initial decision when he is the presiding officer, which stands unless reviewed by the agency; and appeal may, within limits, be taken to the courts.

What is the impact of the Administrative Procedure Act? As noted above, the extensive use of informal procedure negates many of the objectives of the Act. Further, the APA itself contains numerous escape clauses that lead to the exemption of large portions of the administrative process. The wording is ambiguous, and in interpreting the Act the courts have adopted a point of view that generally favors greater rather than less administrative discretion. The ineffectiveness of the APA illustrates the limitation of statutes as instruments to change decision processes that are deeply rooted in the political system. As an attempt to mold the administrative process in the image of the courts the APA was destined to fail.

One of the most interesting aspects of the APA is its establishment of an independent class of hearing examiners. This has been done in conjunction with the separation of prosecuting and adjudicative functions. What this means is that the hearing examiners are not subject to agency control either with respect to their job status or their conduct in relation to the cases they initially decide. When a lawyer takes a case to a hearing examiner he enters a decision process outside the agency's sphere. This practice is based upon the judicial model, which requires personal (as opposed to institutional) and independent judgment in the determination of individual rights and obligations. The problem in the implementation of this practice in the administrative process is that the APA permits the agencies to overrule their examiners whenever they are so inclined. This may seem rather strange, and the question may legitimately be asked, why bother to give the examiners independence under such circumstances; that is, why make their decisions only initially independent? The essential reason was the expectation that a good many examiners' decisions would not be appealed to or taken by the agencies for review. If this were the situation, *de facto* power would reside with the examiners regardless of the ability of the agencies to review *de jure.* These hopeful expectations have not been realized, and it is a common practice for the agencies to overrule their own examiners.

The very fact that the examiners are independent often causes the agencies to reverse or change their own examiners' decisions. Louis J. Hector, a former member of the Civil Aeronautics Board, noted this in testimony before the Senate Subcommittee on Administrative Practice and Procedure of the Judiciary Committee in 1960:

> The hearing examiner who heard the *Seven States* case did not know what the [Civil Aeronautics] Board had in mind in terms of extent of service.
>
> The Board had in its own thinking come around to the conclusion that any town which had any reasonable chance of producing 5 passengers a day should have a chance to see if it could do so, and if it could then it should have an airline.
>
> The hearing examiner did not know this, because he is independent, and the Board could not talk to him.
>
> So he spent two years hearing evidence and turning out a 500-odd page opinion.
>
> It came up to the Board, and the Board's first reaction was, "This wasn't what we had in mind at all. We were thinking of a much more extensive route pattern." [18]

Mr. Hector's remarks vividly illustrate the paradox of trying to establish administrative justice through a separation of policy making and adjudication within the agencies. If an agency is to implement policy, it must be able to control adjudication within its jurisdiction; policy considerations must always be part of the process of adjudication. It is actually impossible to separate the two areas without causing a power struggle between those who are presumably to be policy makers, and those who are to adjudicate individual cases. The historical struggle between the courts and the agencies illustrates the point.

At the present time the limitations of the Administrative Procedure Act are well recognized, but officially the American Bar Association still is attempting to establish greater formalization

18. *Hearings pursuant to S. Res. 234 Before the Subcommittee on Administrative Practice and Procedure of the Senate Committee on the Judiciary,* 86th Cong., 2nd Sess., pp. 231–232 (1960).

of the administrative process along judicial lines. It has recommended the passage of a new Code of Federal Administrative Procedure, which would tighten the procedural requirements of the APA and eliminate most of the exemptions to the Act.[19] The Code would also make it more difficult for the agencies to overrule the decisions of their examiners. In addition to proposing the enactment of the Code, the American Bar Association has recommended the creation of administrative courts that would be entirely separate from the administrative process in several fields.

But formalization of procedure touches only a part of the administrative process. As far as administrative courts are concerned, if they had real adjudicative power they would by definition possess more significant policy power than an administrative agency in the same jurisdiction. A transfer of judicial power means a transfer of policy power. The same problem arises from the Code's provisions giving greater power to hearing examiners than is now the case.

## The Nature of Judicial Review

Aside from attempting to mold internal administrative procedure to conform to the judicial model, the American Bar Association has consistently tried to increase the statutory scope of judicial review and make it more readily available to parties aggrieved by the action of any agency. The courts, however, have been very reluctant to accept broad responsibilities to control the agencies. They have consistently attempted to limit their role in judicial review of administrative decisions.

It seems to be commonly assumed that virtually any group or individual affected adversely by administrative action can obtain review in the courts. Nothing could be further from the truth. Probably the principal reason for this is the inability and lack of willingness of the courts to perform that function on a broad scale. The courts can be extraordinarily powerful when they so desire. Their greatest limitation is *self-restraint*, and not control imposed from outside. For example, for many years the courts

19. For the text of the proposed Code see S. 1887, 87th Cong., 1st Sess. (1961).

refused to consider what they termed "political questions," e.g., problems of reapportionment of state legislatures. The doctrine of limitation kept them out of political controversies that might have proved too much for them to handle. After accepting this doctrine for years, the Supreme Court suddenly changed its mind in 1962 in the case of *Baker v. Carr*, and held that a Federal District Court in Tennessee had jurisdiction to determine whether or not the Tennessee Apportionment Act of 1901 violated any constitutional rights.[20] Space does not permit an examination of the intricacies of judicial decision making, but it should be noted that the law is far from scientific. It must be interpreted by judges; thus, definitions of the nature of statutory or constitutional law will vary from one judge to another, among different courts, and from one generation to the next.

Although the law is uncertain, some fairly consistent patterns have emerged in doctrines of judicial review of administrative decisions. First, the right to review stems from both statutory and constitutional law, although more from the former than the latter. The statutes governing agency procedure contain provisions which either explicitly grant judicial review to parties aggrieved by agency action, preclude review completely, or simply fail to mention the subject. Where explicit provisions exist for review the courts designated by the statute must act as initial appellate bodies. Where there is preclusion of judicial review, the courts will receive a case only if they feel there is a *constitutional* right involved, which would be an extraordinary situation in terms of prevailing judicial practice. Finally, where statutes fail to provide explicit provisions either for or against review, the courts can decide either way. It is difficult to generalize about judicial practice in this twilight zone. The weight of scholarly opinion would probably support the statement that the courts generally will review administrative decisions in the absence of explicit statutory provisions. On the other hand, a very good argument can be made against this point of view. In many extremely important cases the courts have held they have no power to challenge an agency's action because of the lack of affirmative statutory power to that effect.

The Administrative Procedure Act contains various provisions

20. *Baker v. Carr*, 369 U.S. 186 (1962).

relating to judicial review, but the problem in this area as in others is the ambiguous wording of the Act. It provides that "except so far as (1) statutes preclude judicial review or (2) agency action is by law committed to agency discretion—any person suffering legal wrong because of any agency action, or adversely affected or aggrieved by such action within the meaning of any relevant statute, shall be entitled to judicial review thereof." [21] Within the limitations noted, the Administrative Procedure Act prescribes additional requirements for court review; in particular it provides that upon review the whole record of the agency proceedings must be taken into account. It is very easy for a court that is reluctant to review an administrative decision to find statutory *intent* to preclude review even if there is no express statement to that effect; and it is even easier to find that a particular matter is within the discretion of the agency. Such statutory vagueness leads to broad judicial discretion, which more frequently than not means deference to the judgment of the agencies.

As an illustration of the problem of preclusion of judicial review, consider the case of *Schilling v. Rogers* decided by the Supreme Court in 1960 after an appeal from the Court of Appeals for the District of Columbia.[22] Briefly, the case involved a petition by one Schilling, a German alien, to the Office of Alien Property under the Attorney General for the return of certain property that he had owned during World War II, before it was confiscated by the Federal government. The relevant statute was the Trading with the Enemy Act which authorized such a return when certain conditions were met. Citizens of enemy countries, like Schilling, were ineligible unless they could demonstrate they had been victims of political, racial, or religious persecution. The petitioner claimed the government owed him sixty-eight thousand dollars. He alleged that he had been a victim of political persecution and therefore qualified under the Act even though he had always resided in Germany. The hearing examiner made an initial decision supporting Schilling's claim, but it was overruled by the Director of the Office of Alien Property and the Attorney General, the latter refusing review. The petitioner sued in the District Court to have the administrative determination reviewed,

21. APA, § 10.
22. 363 U.S. 666 (1960).

and the court refused a government motion to dismiss the complaint for lack of jurisdiction. The government appealed this decision to the Court of Appeals and secured a reversal on the grounds that judicial review was precluded by section 7 (c) of the Trading with the Enemy Act. This section provides that the sole relief to claimants seeking the return of alien property "shall be that provided by the terms of this Act." The Act, however, does not expressly provide for the remedy of judicial review for enemy nationals such as Schilling. The Supreme Court, in affirming the Court of Appeals, held that judicial review was in effect precluded. In addition, the Court held that the administrative action involved was discretionary. On both these counts, the Administrative Procedure Act's provisions relating to judicial review, on which Schilling had primarily relied, were held inapplicable.

*Schilling v. Rogers* provides some idea of the complexities of getting a court to hear a case in the first place on appeal from the decision of an administrative agency. The next question that must be answered is, what are the courts likely to do if they find that they have jurisdiction to review an administrative decision? What is their power with respect to the agencies, and what is the *scope* of their review? Basically, the powers of the courts over the agencies are defined in the statutes governing both these branches of government, but particularly the agencies themselves. For example, courts may in some instances enjoin administrative action concerning a private party pending the outcome of a court hearing; they may be given the power to remand a case to an agency to carry out the judgment of the court, which may reverse that of the agency in whole or in part; they may remand a case to an agency for rehearing, and so on. In other words the courts have numerous courses of action, most of which are fairly specifically outlined in statutory law.

The courts also attempt to limit rather drastically the issues they will review on appeal from administrative agencies. Statutory law is also relevant here, and may virtually preclude judicial review by narrowly prescribing what the courts can consider. The most extreme case is when a statute states that the findings of fact and of law made by a particular agency shall be final, which means that even though a case may be taken to court the decision of the agency is certain to prevail in virtually every instance. The

Veterans Administration is a good example of such an agency; the decisions of the Administrator of Veterans' Affairs are "final and conclusive on all questions of law and fact, and no other official or court of the United States shall have jurisidiction to review by mandamus or otherwise any such decision." [23] Here statutory preclusion of review is combined with finality of the administrator's decision on the issues. A statutory provision that gives finality to the findings of fact and law of an administrative agency automatically results in preclusion of review unless there is a compelling constitutional question involved.

Judicial self-restraint is particularly strong in the area of review of agency rulings. Without going into the complexities of the subject, it is necessary to note that the courts are more concerned with the *procedural* aspects of a case rather than the substantive aspects, which is simply because the former (points of law) are more within the range of judicial competence than the latter (policy questions and points of fact). The courts have no desire to replace the agencies, but only to make certain they do not stray too far beyond the boundaries of their legal and constitutional authority.

23. 49 Stat. 9 (1934).

# Chapter 4   The Bureaucracy and Congress

ARTICLE I, section 1 of the Constitution states that "all legislative powers herein granted shall be vested in a Congress of the United States, which shall consist of a Senate and House of Representatives." Section 8 enumerates congressional powers and provides that Congress shall have all powers "necessary and proper" to implement them. These provisions are used to justify the establishment of administrative agencies, which become in effect instruments of congressional policy. Congress, however, is supposed to control the agencies it creates, for the Constitution clearly indicates that primary legislative power is to reside in the Senate and the House of Representatives. In Chapter 2 the outlines of congressional-administrative interaction were suggested; particular emphasis was placed on the reasons behind the decisions of Congress to create agencies and delegate substantial authority to them. The purpose of this chapter is to consider congressional-administrative interaction in more precise detail. Four areas of political concern will be assessed. First, the constitutional problem of delegation of legislative power to administrative agencies directly or through the President; second, the role of the bureaucracy in the exercise of functions that were to reside in the legislature; third, the way in which the bureaucracy directly influences Congress in the legislative process through lobbying and propaganda; fourth, the implications of the legislative activities of administrative agencies in terms of the American constitutional system.

## The Delegation of Legislative Power

In Chapter 3 the nature of judicial review of administrative decisions was discussed, and it was pointed out that for the most part the courts have retreated from exercising meaningful review through the adoption of doctrines that permit wide administrative discretion. In no area is this more apparent than in the delegation of legislative power by Congress. The general nature of most congressional bills that concern the implementation of regulatory and other programs by administrative agencies has been noted. The question posed here is exactly how broad can such congressional delegation be and still conform to constitutional standards? In analyzing this question it is necessary to turn to judicial interpretation of the Constitution regarding the delegation of power.

### THE CONSTITUTIONAL PROBLEM

The nature of the constitutional problem can be explained briefly. First, primary legislative power is supposed to reside in Congress under Article I. What constitutes "primary" legislative power in a particular policy area requires interpretation of the Constitution, and therefore becomes the responsibility of the judiciary. Congress can not by itself determine the kinds of delegations it may make because the over-all determination involves constitutional criteria; since *Marbury v. Madison* (1803) this has been considered the province of the courts. If Congress does not set limits to the legislative power it delegates to the agencies or the President, the courts may declare such statutes unconstitutional and thus null and void. The only notable cases in which this was done occurred during the New Deal period. Since the beginning of World War II every instance of congressional delegation to the President or the administrative branch has been upheld.

The central position of the judiciary in formulating standards for the delegation of legislative powers means that decisions can only be made if a case and controversy exists.[1] Any discussion of legal and constitutional doctrine centers upon specific instances of administrative adjudication that subsequently reach the courts. The private party wishing to challenge a particular congressional delegation must first be involved in a reviewable case before the agency to which the delegation has been made. The judiciary

1. *Muskrat v. United States,* 219 U.S. 346 (1911); *United Public Workers v. Mitchell,* 330 U.S. 75 (1947).

will not render advisory opinions on the validity of general administrative policy decisions. When such policy is implemented in a specific case affecting the rights and obligations of private or governmental parties the situation ceases to be advisory. Upon appeal the case may be reviewed by the judiciary.

As a result of the case and controversy requirement for judicial action, the question of delegation of legislative power is narrowed in two directions. First, although administrative legislation is implemented through adjudication, many instances of such adjudication are not subject to judicial review. What may be a case and controversy in the general sense may not conform to judicial criteria.[2] Other problems, such as time, expense, and administrative sanctions may prevent review. Second, the courts will usually not review *substantive* policy issues except as they relate to questions of legal and constitutional *procedure*. Thus, problems concerning the delegation of legislative power do not involve as a general rule what policies Congress has adopted, but whether or not the policies have been stated clearly enough so that the agencies implementing them and the courts upon review can ascertain congressional intent, and whether the *procedures* Congress has authorized the agencies to employ conform to constitutional standards.[3] Insofar as Congress is concerned, the essential problem of delegation of powers involves the need for congressional retention of control over policy formulation. Primary concern must be focused upon the delegation of legislative power rather than judicial power, except as the latter forms an integral part of the regulatory function.

Theoretically the courts require in the delegation of legislative power that the intent of Congress be stated clearly enough so that *ultra vires* action can be prohibited. That is, if an agency exercising delegated power attempts to act beyond the power conferred upon it by statute the courts must be able to prevent it. The statute in question must, therefore, indicate what Congress wants the agency to do in clear terms so that upon review of a

2. For examples of some of the difficulties that arise in trying to convince the courts that a justicable case and controversy exists see: *FCC v. Saunders Bros. Radio Station,* 309 U.S. 470 (1940); *Perkins v. Lukens Steel Co.,* 310 U.S. 113 (1940); *International Longshoremen's and Warehousemen's Union v. Boyd,* 347 U.S. 222 (1954).

3. See, for example, *Kent v. Dulles,* 357 U.S. 116 (1958).

particular administrative action the courts may be able to say either: "This is permitted by Congress"; or "This action is outside the scope of authority granted by Congress." In this way primary legislative power theoretically remains in Congress. If a constitutional question is involved, the courts can determine *ultra vires* action regardless of statutory language. If a statute is unclear as to the procedural policy to be followed by an agency, and if the agency adopts a procedure which the courts subsequently find to be unconstitutional, the courts will not hold the statute unconstitutional but only the particular agency action. In such a situation the courts will tend to say upon review that they must interpret the intent of Congress to include constitutional procedure where statutory language is vague, otherwise the statute itself is unconstitutional by definition.[4] Actually the courts virtually never declare administrative action unconstitutional on the basis of internal agency procedure. Judicial practice in this area can best be shown by a few concrete cases.

Prior to the New Deal period various congressional delegations of power were unsuccessfully attacked as unconstitutional, particularly questions relating to tariffs. It was the practice of Congress to delegate the power to raise or lower tariffs on certain commodities to the President, and in some instances to administrative officials, provided certain conditions existed. For example, the Tariff Act of 1890 gave the President the power to suspend the free introduction of "sugar, molasses, coffee, tea and hides" into the United States if he found that countries producing and exporting these commodities were levying "reciprocally unequal and unreasonable" duties on agricultural or other products from the United States. After such a presidential suspension of free trade in these commodities, certain duties specified by Congress were to go into effect automatically. In 1892 the Supreme Court upheld this delegation of power in stating that "legislative power was exercised when Congress declared that the suspension should take effect upon a named contingency. What the President was required to do was simply in execution of the act of Congress. *It was not the making of law.* He was the mere agent of the lawmaking department to ascertain and declare the event upon which

4. *Ibid.*

its expressed will was to take effect."[5] This was, in fact, a rather narrow delegation in view of what was to come.

The Tariff Act of 1922 gave the President far broader discretion than previous legislation to adjust tariffs whenever he found differences in production costs between the United States and competing foreign countries. Needless to say the Act did in fact give him law making power; however the Supreme Court, recognizing the need for such presidential power, found that this was not an unconstitutional delegation.[6] Since the New Deal, Congress has virtually abdicated its legislative power in the tariff field and given the President and the Tariff Commission the primary responsibility in the establishment of tariffs. The passage of the Trade Expansion Act of 1962 represented a major increase in presidential discretion in this area, not only in relation to Congress but also with respect to the Tariff Commission. Thus for a long period of time Congress has not chosen to exercise effective law making power in the tariff field, although by means of cumbersome procedure it has a veto power. The tariff field is typical of many, and illustrates the complete change that has taken place since the framing of the Constitution between the President and the administrative branch on the one hand, and Congress on the other. The former in combination initiate most legislation, while the latter may veto. A congressional veto, however, is far more difficult to achieve than a presidential veto, for Congess can not for the most part act as a cohesive unit.

UNCONSTITUTIONAL DELEGATIONS OF POWER

The only cases in which the Supreme Court held congressional statutes unconstitutional on the basis of undue delegation of legislative power occurred during the New Deal. The fact that the Court was openly hostile to President Roosevelt's political goals has caused some observers to feel that the Court often acted from political bias when it ruled much of the New Deal legislation unconstitutional. This point of view is supported by the extraordinary delegations that occurred after the 1937 attempt by Roosevelt to

5. *Field v. Clark*, 143 U.S. 649, 693 (1892). Italics added.
6. *J. W. Hampton, Jr. & Co. v. United States*, 276 U.S. 394 (1928).

"pack" the court.

The New Deal legislation which delegated too much legislative power was the famous, and perhaps notorious, National Industrial Recovery Act of 1933. Section I contained a congressional "declaration of policy," couched in vague terminology, that declared a national emergency to exist and stated that it was the policy of Congress to increase the flow and amount of interstate and foreign commerce through various devices, including greater cooperation among groups within particular industries. The Act then went on to delegate the power to implement its vague policy standards to the President and subordinate agencies or officials designated by him. Section III gave him virtually complete discretion to establish codes of fair competition within industries if he felt them to be warranted by prevailing economic conditions. There was really no check upon his power in this respect, for the policy directives of Congress were worded so that they could be interpreted almost in any way. This Act affected powerful private interests, and they soon sought relief in the courts from presidential and agency action that had been taken under its authority. In 1935, the Supreme Court struck down a section of the Act for unconstitutional delegation of legislative power in *Panama Refining Co. v. Ryan;* [7] later that year, in the historic case of *Schechter Poultry Corp. v. United States,* it declared the entire Act unconstitutional on the same basis.[8] In the latter decision the Court examined the provisions of the Act in detail and unanimously found that

. . . Section 3 of the Recovery Act is without precedent. It supplies no standards for any trade, industry or activity. It does not undertake to prescribe rules of conduct to be applied to particular states of fact determined by appropriate administrative procedure. Instead of prescribing rules of conduct, it authorizes the making of codes to prescribe them. For that legislative undertaking, section 3 sets up no standards, aside from the statement of the general aims of rehabilitation, correction and expansion described in section one. In view of the scope of that broad declaration, and of the nature of the few restrictions that are imposed, the discretion of the President in approving or prescribing codes, and thus enacting laws for the government of

7.  293 U.S. 388 (1935).
8.  295 U.S. 495 (1935).

trade and industry throughout the country, is virtually unfettered. We think that the code-making authority thus conferred is an unconstitutional delegation of power. . . .[9]

The scope of this Act was too much even for those on the Court sympathetic to the purposes of the New Deal and willing to allow flexible congressional delegations.

In what respect does the delegation of legislative power in the National Industrial Recovery Act of 1933 differ from previous and subsequent delegations, all of which have been held constitutional? In some respects the delegation held unconstitutional in *Schechter* was actually broader and more unlimited than that found in most subsequent and previous congressional statutes. This idea is best supported by the concurring opinion of Justice Cardozo in the *Schechter* case. He had previously disagreed with the majority of the Court in the *Panama* case; he found in the section of the Recovery Act in question adequate standards expressed by Congress to support the delegation of power that had been made to the President.[10] He supported the idea of flexible criteria as adequate to justify the delegation of legislative power; however, with respect to Section III of the Recovery Act and the powers it conferred he noted:

. . . Here . . . is an attempted delegation not confined to any single act nor to any class or group of acts identified or described by reference to a standard. Here in effect is a roving commission to inquire into evils and upon discovery correct them.

I have said that there is no standard, definite or even approximate, to which legislation must conform. Let me make my meaning more precise. If codes of fair competition are codes eliminating "unfair" methods of competition ascertained upon inquiry to prevail in one industry or another, there is no unlawful delegation of legislative functions when the President is directed to inquire into such practices and denounce them when discovered. For many years a like power has been committed to the Federal Trade Commission with the approval of this court in a long series of decisions . . . . Delegation in such circumstances is born of the necessities of the occasion. The industries of the country are too many and diverse to make it possible for Congress, in respect of matters such as these, to legislate

9. *Ibid.*, pp. 541–542.
10. 293 U.S. 388, 434–435 (1935).

directly with adequate appreciation of varying conditions. . . .

But there is another conception of codes of fair competition . . . [by which] a code is not to be restricted to the elimination of business practices that would be characterized by general acceptance as oppressive or unfair. It is to include whatever ordinances may be desirable or helpful for the well-being or prosperity of the industry affected. In that view, the function of its adoption is not merely negative, but positive; the planning of improvements as well as the extirpation of abuses. What is fair, as thus conceived, is not something to be contrasted with what is unfair or fraudulent or tricky. The extension becomes as wide as the field of industrial regulation. If that conception shall prevail, anything that Congress may do within the limits of the commerce clause for the betterment of business may be done by the President upon the recommendation of a trade association [or through independent presidential action] by calling it a code. This is delegation running riot. No such plenitude of power is susceptible of transfer. The statute, however, aims at nothing less, as one can learn both from its terms and from the administrative practice under it. . . .[11]

To Cardozo the Recovery Act meant a virtual abdication of congressional power in the economic sphere.

THE SCOPE OF DELEGATED POWER SINCE THE NEW DEAL

Since the New Deal extraordinary delegations have taken place, particularly during the World War II era; however, relative to the kind of delegation that Congress attempted in the Recovery Act of 1933, these later delegations have been limited in several respects. In general, the scope of administrative power is curtailed in congressional delegation. Standards of delegation are always vague and result in a great deal of administrative discretion, but usually the area of discretion has boundaries: this is the first limiting factor. Agencies can not rove about from one field to another and prescribe legislation wherever it is considered to be necessary. For example, the Interstate Commerce Commission is limited to the rail, trucking, and certain aspects of the shipping industries; the Federal Communications Commission is limited to the radio, television, telegraph and telephone industries. Most other regulatory and nonregulatory agencies have reasonably definite

11. 295 U.S. 495, 551–553 (1935).

jurisdictions.

An additional restraint results from the fact that it is quite common for the agencies themselves to prescribe standards that are self-limiting. If an agency takes action that violates its own standards a court upon review quite likely will invalidate the action and remand the case to the agency. In this respect the courts have taken the position that it is not always necessary for Congress to set forth in detail standards to guide administrative agencies in exercising delegated power, but that it is important for such standards to emanate from some source—usually the agencies themselves.[12] The theory behind this requirement is that as long as criteria exist governing agency activity the bureaucracy will be limited. The problem is, however, that Congress is not the primary source of limitation; thus, the theory that Congress must retain primary legislative power has been substantially altered in practice with the growth of bureaucracy. To a considerable extent the delegation of power doctrine requiring a clear statement of legislative intent has shifted to require simply that administrative action be limited in some way through the establishment of standards which may or may not be congressional in origin.

A virtual abdication of congressional power to the President and the administrative branch was brought about by World War II. Extraordinary delegations were made and upheld by the courts, and it was during this period that the substitution of administrative for congressional standards was allowed. For example, the Emergency Price Control Act of 1942 authorized a Price Administrator, who was to be head of the Office of Price Administration (OPA), to fix prices for commodities, rents, and services which "in his judgment will be generally fair and equitable and will effectuate the purposes of this Act." The purposes of the Act were "to stabilize prices and to prevent speculative, unwarranted, and abnormal increases in prices and rents. . . ." The Administrator was "so far as practicable" to consult with representatives of the industries and to "give due consideration to the prices prevailing between October 1 and October 15,

12. See Henry J. Friendly, *The Federal Administrative Agencies* (Cambridge: Harvard University Press, 1962) for a detailed consideration of the importance of administrative standards.

1941." In 1944 the Supreme Court upheld this delegation of power in *Yakus v. United States* with the statement that

it is for Congress to say whether the data on the basis of which prices are to be fixed are to be confined within a narrow or a broad range. In either case the only concern of courts is to ascertain whether the will of Congress has been obeyed. This depends not upon the breadth of the definition of the facts or conditions which the administrative officer is to find but upon the determination whether the definition sufficiently *marks the field* within which the Administrator is to act so that it may be known whether he has kept within it in compliance with the legislative will.[13]

Further,

the standards prescribed by the present Act, *with the aid of* the 'statement of considerations' required to be made by the Administrator, are sufficiently definite and precise to enable Congress, the courts and the public to ascertain whether the Administrator, in fixing the designated prices, has conformed to those standards.[14]

Justice Roberts dissented in *Yakus,* objecting to what he considered an unconstitutional delegation of legislative power. Roberts stated that in his opinion *Yakus* clearly overruled *Schechter,* and that in fact there was little difference in the extent of delegation that took place under the statutes involved in these cases. Although an argument can be made for this point of view, it is probably more correct to say that relative to the Recovery Act, the Emergency Price Control Act of 1942 represented a narrower delegation of congressional power. In the Recovery Act the ability of the President, or an administrator designated by him, to effect "codes of fair competition" encompassed virtually any action that could be taken. It authorized price setting and general control of labor relations and business practices. The Emergency Price Control Act was limited to price setting; hence the field of administrative jurisdiction as well as the specific powers that could be exercised by the OPA were designated. Within this field the OPA possessed what amounted to virtually total discretion, but in this respect it is similar to many administrative agencies.

13. *Yakus v. United States,* 321 U.S. 414, 425 (1944). Italics added.
14. *Ibid.,* p. 426. Italics added.

In addition to the Emergency Price Control Act of 1942, other World War II statutes were challenged as being unconstitutional delegations of legislative power, but in every instance they were upheld in the Supreme Court.[15] Similarly, most of the delegations of power made by Congress to the various regulatory agencies have been challenged and upheld consistently by the judiciary.[16] Where does this leave us today? Does it mean that any transference of power from Congress to the bureaucracy will not meet constitutional or legal obstacles? In general terms, this conclusion is accurate. The necessity of broad administrative discretion in the legislative area is recognized. There is simply no other way to conduct the business of government given its present scope and complexity. Although many congressmen consider the agencies to be "agents of Congress" when they exercise legislative functions, the vagueness of statutory terminology, the leniency and limitations of the courts in controlling standards of delegation, and the political difficulties Congress faces in attempting to control the agencies once they have been given legislative and other powers, all indicate administrative domination of the legislative sphere.

In addition to the regulatory statutes, delegation from Congress to the agencies is equally broad; a typical example may be found in the legislation governing the Defense Department. Congress has authorized the Secretary of the Army to:

. . . procure materials and facilities necessary to maintain and support the Army, its military organizations, and their installations and supporting and auxiliary elements, including:
   (1) guided missiles;
   (2) modern standard items of equipment;
   (3) equipment to replace obsolete or unserviceable equipment;
   (4) necessary spare equipment, materials, and parts; and
   (5) such reserve of supplies as is needed to enable the Army to perform its mission.[17]

15. For an example of virtually uncontrolled delegation of legislative power during the war see *Lichter v. United States*, 334 U.S. 742 (1948).
16. For examples see *ICC v. Brimson*, 154 U.S. 447 (1894); *New York Central Securities Corp. v. United States*, 287 U.S. 12 (1932); *Federal Radio Commission v. General Electric*, 281 U.S. 464 (1930).
17. 10 U.S.C. 4531. 70A Stat. 253 (1956).

The Secretary of the Air Force is directed to purchase necessary aircraft or airframe tons to maintain superiority in the air; this essentially constitutes congressional intent as it is stated in the relevant statutes. The Secretary of the Navy has equally broad discretion; all three Secretaries are now subordinate to the Secretary of Defense. The same kind of congressional delegation is common outside the realm of defense policy; it would be called extraordinary except for the fact that it has become the rule rather than the exception.

It is possible to conclude that there are no constitutional or legal restrictions that have impeded in any substantial way the trend toward greater delegation. This situation has not, of course, resulted from administrative usurpation, but from congressional desire. It is a necessary attribute of the modern democratic state.

## The Bureaucracy and Legislation

Normally, the legislative process is thought of in terms of Congress and congressional committees, the President, and political parties. The bureaucracy is always considered a factor in legislative formulation, but more often than not it is felt to be appropriately placed in the background. This is because the idea of a neutral civil service under the control of both the President and Congress is generally accepted. The fact, already suggested, that the administrative branch is neither neutral nor controlled in any substantial way can now be elaborated.

### ADMINISTRATIVE RULE MAKING

Administrative agencies were in many instances created both to formulate legislation through rule making and to recommend legislative proposals to Congress. Rule making involves filling in the details of congressional enactments, which administrative agencies are generally empowered to do on their own initiative. The actual volume of rule making, which governs the day-to-day activities of groups subject to government regulation, far exceeds the business of Congress and constitutes in many areas the life-blood of the legislative process. Influence from the outside upon administrative rule making is necessarily limited and sporadic.

A few examples should serve to indicate the importance of rule making by the bureaucracy. The Federal Trade Commission Act of 1914 states (§ 5) that "unfair methods of competition in commerce, and unfair or deceptive acts or practices in commerce, are hereby declared unlawful." Further, the Act provides that the "Commission is hereby empowered and directed to prevent persons, partnerships, or corporations . . . from using unfair methods of competition in commerce and unfair or deceptive acts or practices in commerce." What is an "unfair" method of competition? Congress does not say in the Federal Trade Commission Act, nor do other acts shed much light on the subject. The Clayton Act, for example, contains more detailed provisions but the wording is such that the Federal Trade Commission, charged with the administration of this Act along with other agencies, still possesses virtually complete discretion in formulating rules under it. The last chapter pointed out the ways agencies differ in their interpretation of the anti-trust laws (the *El Paso Natural Gas* case), a situation which follows from the failure of Congress to lay down specific rules in most regulatory fields.

Although the Clayton Act was to be a more precise indication of congressional policy in the anti-trust field than the Sherman Act or the Federal Trade Commission Act, it was couched in language that was anything but clear, a passage from Section 2 will illustrate:

. . . [I]t shall be unlawful for any person engaged in commerce, in the course of such commerce, either directly or indirectly, to discriminate in price between different purchasers of commodities of like grade and quality, where either or any of the purchases involved in such discrimination are in commerce, where such commodities are sold for use, consumption, or resale within the United States or any Territory thereof or the District of Columbia or any insular possession or other place under the jurisdiction of the United States, and where the effect of such discrimination may be substantially to lessen competition or tend to create a monopoly in any line of commerce, or to injure, destroy, or prevent competition with any person who either grants or knowingly receives the benefit of such discrimination, or with customers of either of them: *Provided,* that nothing herein contained shall prevent differentials which make only due allowance for differences in the cost of manufacture, sale, or delivery resulting from the differing methods or quantities in which such commodities are to such purchasers sold or delivered: *Provided however,* that the Federal Trade Commission may, after due investigation and hearing to all interested parties, fix and establish quantity limits, and revise the same as it finds necessary, as to particular commodities or classes of commodities, where it finds that available purchasers in greater quantities are so few as to render differentials on account thereof unjustly discriminatory or promotive of monopoly in any line of commerce; and the foregoing shall then not be construed to permit differentials based on differences in quantities greater than those so fixed and established. . . .

This statute is not cited to confuse but to illuminate. It may look fairly precise on the surface; however, more careful observation reveals that the entire effect of this section depends upon *administrative interpretation* of imprecise and vague terminology. After initial agency interpretation of such words as "discriminate," "competition," and "monopoly" the meaning of anti-trust policy is shaped, subject of course to final judicial approval. Thus, if one seeks to determine the nature of anti-trust policy in the United States, greater attention has to be given to administrative and judicial policy directives and decisions than to congressional enactments.

Many of the factors that give the bureaucracy a vital part in the formulation of regulatory policy cause the same result in non-regulatory fields. In military and foreign policy formulation the President has important constitutional as well as statutory responsibilities, which give his office a far greater role than it has in most domestic policy areas; therefore regulatory and nonregulatory fields differ in the degree of involvement of the agencies in policy formulation. The fact that the President participates to a substantial degree in many policy fields does not, however, necessarily detract from the importance of the bureaucracy. In fact it may enhance the influence of the agencies, particularly if they can swing the President to their point of view and thus gain additional political support for their programs. The Defense Department provides an excellent example of an administrative agency (or agencies) that exercises controlling influence in military policy formulation in that the President generally goes along with it; in some instances it influences even in spite of presidential opposition.

## Reasons for Administrative Domination
## in the Legislative Process

What leads to the power to formulate public policy in a developed governmental system generally?

### CONSTITUTIONAL AND LEGAL AUTHORITY

First, to make public policy or legislate, which are both the same thing generically, a governmental group, whether in the legislative, executive (administrative), or judicial branch, must possess constitutional and legal authority. Statutory authority to legislate is given in very broad terms by Congress to the President and the bureaucracy; thus, there is no lack of legal authority in the administrative branch. The conclusion that may be reached is that at the present time Congress and the bureaucracy possess roughly equal constitutional and legal authority to legislate. Congress can theoretically take this authority away from the administrative agencies, though it would never do so because of the very reasons that have necessitated the rise of administrative policy formulation in the first place. To renounce the role of the bureaucracy in legislation would be essentially the same thing as abolishing the administrative branch almost completely, which is neither practically nor politically possible.

### ORGANIZATIONAL PATTERNS AND POLITICAL SUPPORT

Second, the ability to formulate policy depends upon organizational patterns and the attainment of *political support,* and here are the most important clues to explain administrative power over legislation. Congress operates through the committee system, and the chairmen of committees are focal points in the decision process. But the committees cannot by themselves generate enough support to pass legislation except in rare instances, although they can delay the consideration of particular bills. There is really no group within Congress that controls the decision process, since the party system is weak at the national level. Thus Congress can not act as a unit through a party majority in either house, and patterns of political support for any congressionally sponsored policy are changeable and diffuse.

Proposed congressional bills must first gain support within the appropriate committees in both houses. Then they must be reported on and passed by the entire body, which is split into two separate groups that are frequently in conflict, the House and Senate. In order for a bill to pass there must be outside political support favoring it. Where will such support materialize? Constituents acting as individuals are not as important as organized group support of congressional decision making; hence, a balance of interest group support must generally be attained before Congress can act. This fact, in addition to the battle for political survival that most congressmen must engage in, results in a network of relationships that are established among particular congressmen and congressional committees, and outside groups and key individuals in the elites of these groups. One of the best sources of political support is to be found in the administrative agencies concerned with the desired legislation, for these agencies constitute the key interest groups in the majority of cases.

The bureaucracy, like Congress, must also obtain political support before embarking upon new legislative programs, but in many instances it either already possesses such support from clientele groups or has the tools to achieve it without much trouble. Administrative policies often have virtually automatic political support which will in turn have significant impact upon Congress, for the groups that support the bureaucracy are more frequently than not very powerful economically and politically.

If an administrative agency wants to embark upon a new policy that is not immediately popular politically, it will have to employ various devices to secure political backing. But even then it is in a better position than the groups within Congress that may also want to innovate, because administrative agencies have greater power, and each possesses by itself greater ability to act as a unit than Congress, which must act through congressional committees and individual congressmen. If the Defense Department wants to cut back on the RS-70 bomber program, a vital decision (and at the time it was made a new departure in defense policy), an administrative directive is issued to this effect, and unless overwhelming political opposition is encountered the order is carried out. The Defense Department controls the expenditure of vast sums of money and hence groups within the armaments industry are in particular instances more or less at the mercy of defense officials. As a whole the Department must maintain general political support, but this is not difficult. Although some industry groups may be unhappy about the curtailment of programs directly affecting them, there are always others that benefit. On balance the Defense Department has automatic political support for virtually anything it wants to do, provided the total defense budget remains roughly the same or increases. Through a vigorous Secretary of Defense it possesses the ability to act rapidly and with firmness in the formulation of policy, whereas Congress, because of its diffuse internal power structure, can not act in the same way even if it possesses the information to make complex policy decisions, which is not always the case.

## THE CASE OF THE RS-70 BOMBER PROGRAM

To illustrate in relative terms the roles of Congress and the bureaucracy in relation to problems of political support and organizational patterns the case of the cutback in the RS-70 (called originally the B-70) bomber program that took place in 1962, to take effect in the 1963 fiscal year budget, is instructive. Powerful congressmen—in particular Carl Vinson of Georgia, chairman of the House Armed Services Committee—the Defense Department, and the President became involved. The case centered upon an executive-legislative struggle to control a military budget item that provided funds for the development of the RS-70. One of the most important powers Congress can exert to control the administrative branch is thought by many to be the power of appropriation of money. In the past this control over the purse was feared and was an important reason why Madison and Hamilton in *The Federalist* and others at the time felt Congress would dominate the coordinate branches of government. After all, without money the bureaucracy, the President, and the judicial branch would be powerless. For this reason the Constitution states that both the President and the Supreme Court Justices shall at least receive compensation for their services which shall not be reduced during their continuance in office. But appropriations are vital to far more areas than salaries. In these areas Congress can do anything it wishes; thus, it theoretically can easily bring coordinate branches into line through the threat of removal of a portion or all of their appropriations.

Although this argument sounds reasonable, the fact is that the scope and complexity of modern government has resulted in the transference of the bulk of the budgetary power to the President and the administrative branch. The budget is formulated for the most part by the powerful Bureau of the Budget in conjunction with the President and the agencies, and then submitted to Congress for approval. Congress makes a few changes, usually cutting back in areas where there is a lack of strong political opposition to reductions, as in the case of foreign aid; however, for the most part the President's budget is not significantly altered. Only a handful of congressmen have the time or energy to read the budget, which is extraordinarily bulky. Even small appropriation bills run to several hundred pages, whereas the total budget is equivalent to thousands of pages. The skill and effort that the administrative branch puts into the formulation of a budget are generally respected in congressional quarters, where there is neither the staff nor the time for adequate review. In 1962 a defense appropriation of close to fifty billion dollars was passed in the House of Representatives unanimously in a matter of a few minutes. This may be extreme, but for the most part it is an accurate reflection of congressional response to budget proposals from the President.

The case of the RS-70 involved a relatively small amount of money, but it illustrates the broad problem of executive-legislative relations. In formulating the military budget for the fiscal year ending June 30, 1963, Secretary of Defense Robert McNamara and his advisers in conjunction with the President proposed that funds for the development of a supersonic bomber, called the RS-70 ("reconnaissance strike"), be drastically cut and that the plans for production of the bomber on a mass scale be dropped entirely. This was in line with a shift in defense policy toward greater reliance upon missiles for both offensive and defensive purposes. McNamara had nothing against manned bombers as such, but he felt that a changing technology was rendering them obsolete. As is always the case when important issues of policy are concerned, powerful individuals and groups both within Congress and the Defense Department itself opposed his decision. The Secretary of Defense always has to contend with his own service chiefs, as well as with key congressmen. In this respect the process of policy formulation is highly political, and the domination of certain policy spheres by the bureaucracy does not in any way eliminate the political factor. Agencies are more frequently than not in conflict with each other, and in the case of large agencies or departments intra-agency political conflict is as acute in many instances as inter-agency conflict.

The decision to reduce manned bombers and the RS-70 in particular met the immediate opposition of Carl Vinson, who has represented Georgia in the House of Representatives since 1914. Vinson is a legend on Capitol Hill, and is reputed to be a powerful influence on the military, not only because he is the chairman of the House Armed Services Committee, but because of his long acquaintance with the military field, which has resulted in a certain degree of inside knowledge as well as close ties with key military figures. He was chairman of the Naval Affairs Committee from 1931 to 1947, and has been chairman of the Armed Services Committee for all but two years since 1949. Regardless of the legend, the fact is that the Armed Services Committees in both the House and the Senate have not been particularly important in military policy formulation in recent years, and with the exception of the areas of manpower and construction, the legislation emanating from these committees gives complete discretion to the military bureaucracy, for the terminology used is typically imprecise and can be interpreted in a variety of ways. Insofar as the RS-70 is concerned, Congressman Vinson was not the only figure opposed to the elimination of the program in 1962. The Air Force, theoretically within the Defense Department and subject to the Secretary's control, also favored a manned bomber buildup, and Air Force Chief of Staff General Curtis LeMay expressed vocal opposition to McNamara's proposals. In addition to Air Force opposition, various congressmen and private groups led by North American Aviation, Inc., which would be adversely affected by the cancellation of military contracts in connection with the program, opposed any cutback.

The general plan of McNamara was initially to allocate 171

million dollars to North American Aviation, Inc., and its subcontractors, to build three test models of the RS-70. This figure was subsequently raised to 223 million dollars. The proponents of the program, spearheaded by Vinson and LeMay, wanted a minimum of 491 million dollars spent the first year, and ultimately 5 to 10 billion dollars. The House of Representatives supported the Defense Department in its final defense appropriation bill, largely because George Mahon, chairman of the powerful Appropriations Subcommittee on Defense, was in favor of this course of action. Vinson and others were unable to overcome the combination of a powerful administrative agency with a powerful congressional committee.

The Senate, on the other hand, did not go along with the Defense Department, and appropriated the 491 million dollars that had been requested for the RS-70. The net result of a divided Congress on this issue was that the Defense Department triumphed by standing on its constitutional right to refuse to spend money appropriated by Congress. Congress may authorize expenditure, but it can do little to bring it about unless it is able to persuade the President and the administrative agencies concerned that its policy position is appropriate. A united Congress has a good chance for success in this endeavor, but a divided legislature has little hope. The Senate-House conference committee on the RS-70 finally authorized the expenditure of 362 million dollars, but McNamara had a tacit agreement with the House conferees that he would not spend the entire appropriation. Thus the House conferees, who supported the Defense Department, agreed to go through the motions of authorizing additional expenditure so that quick agreement could be reached with the Senate. At the same time they recognized that final power resided with the Secretary of Defense, who would use their informal support to implement the program he desired in the first place.

The most notable point illustrated by the RS-70 case is that the general fragmentation of the policy process works to the disadvantage of Congress and groups within Congress relative to the bureaucracy, particularly if the President supports an administrative agency. Many of the constitutional powers of Congress are meaningless in view of the general lack of congressional unity. The fact that there is no consistent and cohesive majority rule in the legislature gives particular agencies far more power than would otherwise be the case. In some instances if there is a balance of power among opposing agencies Congress may swing the decision one way or the other. More often than not, however, the balance is held by the President, who can always act with greater dispatch than Congress. The President acts as a source of political strength in such cases, which, when combined with that of the agencies, often cannot be effectively challenged by Congress.

## CONGRESS AND CONTROL OVER APPROPRIATIONS

So far the factors leading to a domination of the policy or legislative process have been listed as (1) constitutional and statutory authority, (2) political support, and (3) enough organizational unity to take firm action. On balance these factors provide the bureaucracy in combination with the President with far greater power to legislate than Congress. The power to control appropriations, which is frequently discussed separately, is really subsumed by these categories. The actual power of appropriation of money will determine in many instances the policy that will be followed; however, although Congress has constitutional authority in this area the initiative actually resides for the most part in the President and the administrative branch. Within Congress the importance of appropriations gives the Appropriations Committees and subcommittees great weight in the formulation of congressional policy, and causes them to be focal points for political pressure from the administrative branch and other groups concerned with legislation. The military Appropriations Subcommittees, for example, are more important in the formulation of military policy than the Armed Services Committees because the expenditure of money is involved in virtually every area of such policy. Thus in order to determine whether or not an appropriation should be made the validity of particular policies must be ascertained. Nevertheless, these committees act primarily in a reviewing capacity, and have little to do with the initiation of public policy. Even their reviews must necessarily be cursory from an over-all standpoint. They may exhaustively examine particular areas of appropriations and policy, but the time spent so doing precludes meaningful review in other areas. Neither the Appropriations Committees nor any others have the time or the staff necessary to overcome executive and administrative domination of the important policy fields. In the case of the cutback in the RS-70, it is true that Chairman Mahon of the House Appropriations Subcommittee on Defense was in favor of the Defense Department point of view; had he and others on that Committee been in opposition it would not have been as easy for Defense Secretary McNamara to implement his policy. However, this consideration is not as important as the fact that the balance of congressional support is likely to be in favor of policies initiated in the administrative branch because that is where political support, decision making power, and expert knowledge reside.

## INFORMATION AND POLICY MAKING

A final important factor should be noted as a determinant of policy making power: legislation today, in regulatory and non-regulatory fields alike, requires specialized information on the part of policy makers before it can be conceptualized, drafted, and implemented. Policy areas are for the most part highly technical with respect to legal, economic, and political factors. While expert knowledge does not require a Ph.D. in mathematics, engineering or other scientific subjects, nor in the social sciences, it does, on the other hand, demand an intimate acquaintance with the issues that arise in the particular policy areas that are the concern of modern government. It is knowledge that can only be acquired from specialization and experience.

Several problems arise regarding the relationship between information and the policy process. First, because there are numerous areas of specialization it is necessary to have a broad division of labor in government. Second, *within* particular policy fields there are a variety of areas of specialized competence that must be applied before the total picture can be understood. This further expands the division of labor required. Congress attempts to meet this situation through its committee system, which essentially results in dividing the legislative sphere into numerous units that are then assigned to permanent standing committees. Temporary policy problems are met through the creation of *ad hoc* or select committees, which hopefully are disbanded when there is no longer a need for them. These committees have funds to employ a permanent but very small staff; in addition each congressman receives funds to employ assistants for administrative purposes. This is the direct result of the Legislative Reorganization Act of 1946, which its optimistic sponsors hoped would put Congress back in the running against the overriding power of the bureaucracy in legislation.[18]

Although Congress has made strenuous efforts to fulfill its constitutional responsibilities, neither its committees nor its staff aids are any match for the administrative branch with respect to knowledge and information in particular areas of legislation. Much of the staff employed by Congress comes directly from the administrative branch, in which initial competence was acquired in an atmosphere where the points of view of the agencies predominated. Sometimes these viewpoints carry over to congressional staff members. Beyond its own staff, Congress must rely upon information that comes directly from the agencies concerned in particular policy fields. Needless to say, the kinds of information that reach congressional committees and congressmen often determine their attitudes toward policy questions. To a considerable extent when the administrative branch can control the channels of information to Congress it can control the policies supported by that body.

The superiority of the bureaucracy with respect to information stems from several factors. First, in contrast to Congress the administrative branch affords individuals a greater opportunity to specialize in particular areas on a permanent basis. Administrative personnel are able to maintain fairly continuous contact with fields under their jurisdiction without having to face the possibility of losing their jobs at given intervals. Congressmen must enter the electoral process and win in order to survive. They must represent the views of their constituents to a degree sufficient to secure reelection. In the House of Representatives, the two-year electoral cycle requires members to spend a significant portion

18. For the history and purposes of the Legislative Reorganization Act of 1946 see George B. Galloway, *The Legislative Process and Congress* (New York: Thomas Y. Crowell Co., 1955); and Ernest S. Griffith, *Congress—Its Contemporary Role* (3rd ed., New York: New York University Press, 1961), chap. vii.

of their tenure in office campaigning.

Though administrators and administrative agencies also have constituents, they do not have to enter the electoral process, and therefore can react to their constituents in a manner quite different from elected officials. The agencies have more power over their constituents than any individual congressman, and they are not subject to the capricious whims of typical voters. Their political support tends to be more consistent and permanent because the agencies have greater durability than congressional counterparts. Thus, although the bureaucracy must maintain political consent for its actions, it possesses more techniques and time to achieve it than members of Congress.

The electoral process not only results in congressmen spending much of their time campaigning, but profoundly affects the kinds of issues and therefore the types of information with which they must be familiar. Political consent is achieved by congressmen through a proper emphasis upon personal and local issues that, for the most part, are not particularly relevant to national policy. Administrative agencies, on the other hand, achieve consent through the adoption of *policies* that will win the approval of powerful groups within their constituency.

The answer that may be given to the problem of inadequate congressional information in policy fields is to increase staff aids and in addition to put campaigning on the basis of policy issues rather than personalities. There is really no way, however, to accomplish either of these objectives. The staff aids to Congress could not possibly be increased enough to counterbalance the bureaucracy. Even if congressional staff were strengthened at the present time, this would not transform Congress into a dominant and effective legislative body again. The members of Congress would still be relying upon experts, even though they would be their experts. And where are these "experts" supposed to get their information? From those who possess it in the first place, namely the bureaucracy and private interest groups. This is not to say that congressional staff is inexpert in all areas or incompetent in any way; congressional staffs are necessarily divorced from the operational end of agency activity, which separates them from a rich source of knowledge directly relevant to the particular policy fields involved.

As an example of the inadequacy of the congressional staff, consider the Legislative Reference Service. In the Library of Congress, directly across from the Capitol and adjacent to the House office buildings, the Legislative Reference Service occupies a few cramped offices. In one of them are two individuals concerned with the area of military policy. Their skills are bolstered by five or ten more members of the congressional staff who serve committees and congressmen dealing with defense matters. This small band is supposed to provide information to Congress on defense matters so that congressmen can at least ask intelligent questions at hearings that involve the Pentagon staff, military and civilian. Much of what is done in the Pentagon is classified, which poses additional problems to Congress, which may or may not have access to secret information. In any event, obviously the primary source of information for the congressional staff is the Pentagon itself; hence, the information that reaches Congress is likely to come directly or indirectly from the Defense Department even though it has its own staff to deal with these matters.

With respect to increasing the importance of policy issues in political campaigns, this is not in line with the results of recent research into the characteristics of electoral behavior. The voter often is not interested in complex policy matters, and it is no insult to the electorate to say that many areas of policy should not be subject to electoral choice. All of the electorate should not have to debate the merits of one missile as opposed to another in defense policy; nor safety measures in the control of aircraft; nor whether the interest rate should be high or low; nor the level of tariffs, and so forth. Of course matters such as these are always subject to discussion in the electorate; however, the idea that the entire electorate should take an interest in all issues of public policy is obsolete in the modern democratic state. Congress, as one group representing the public, does not have to formulate public policy in every instance in order to conform to a constitutional and democratic system of government. Given the inevitable scope of administrative activity in the legislative field, what functions does Congress fulfill? Where should the line be drawn between permissible administrative discretion in legislation, and congressional control?

## Administrative Lobbying
## and Propaganda

The ability of administrative agencies to marshal support in favor of particular programs is often severely tested, and as a result the agencies have frequently created public relations departments on a permanent basis to engineer consent for their legislative proposals. Administrative personnel engaged in public relations are not so open about their activities as their counterparts in private advertising and public relations firms, for the myth that the bureaucracy is "neutral" must be maintained if possible. However, through what might be called undercover devices, the bureaucracy engages in extensive lobbying and propaganda activities.

The agencies are faced with the problem of engineering consent in Congress, and in those groups under their jurisdiction which are directly affected by their decisions. If these latter groups are powerful the administrative agencies that gain their approval for particular policies will also have automatic congressional support in those quarters to which the groups have access. The entire Congress will not be affected, but key committees dealing in the same areas as the agencies are likely to be persuaded one way or the other if powerful agency clientele groups apply pressure. In some policy fields Congress must act affirmatively to effect the legislative proposals of the bureaucracy. In others, administrative agencies can take action independently; however, in these cases they always face the possibility of adverse congressional and clientele group reaction. Congressional investigations are always unpleasant and they may affect the balance of political support unfavorably if they turn up administrative irregularities.

Administrative agencies function to a considerable extent as freewheeling interest groups, and in their use of propaganda activities they are no exception. They not only seek to apply pressure at critical points in the political process, but also strive to maintain a favorable image of themselves before the public generally and before specific groups which they consider important in the battle for political survival. The armed forces, for example, employ numerous devices, from the recruiting poster to the full-length motion picture, to convey their importance to the public. Particular services, sometimes in conjunction with their clientele groups, attempt to persuade the public, congressmen, and the President of their worth relative to coordinate services. For example Lockheed Aircraft, prime contractor for the Polaris submarine missile, has used its public relations and advertising departments to help publicize the importance of the Navy, while Douglas Aircraft has boosted the Army or the Air Force for which it is building missiles. Defense contractors are often willing to boost any service that uses their products, although of course good relations are maintained with all services, for they too are actual or potential customers. Such activity supplements that of the services and is designed to influence policy makers in the bureaucracy as well as in outside departments and groups. In other words, the bureaucracy lobbies itself in cases where the significant decision making power resides in the administrative branch.

Congress has always been concerned with administrative lobbying and propaganda in much the same way that it has given attention to similar activities in private groups. The Federal Regulation of Lobbying Act of 1946 requires the registration of groups and individuals attempting to influence legislation before Congress, but it applies only to private groups and not to administrative agencies. If General Motors Corporation, for example, tried to lobby Congress in the same manner as the Defense Department, heated objections would be raised. Imagine the President of General Motors personally stalking the halls of Congress to buttonhole key members, with the aid of a staff of several hundred.

Many private groups maintain substantial lobbying staffs in Washington, but they do not have quite the same access and privileges as administrative agencies. They cannot conduct congressmen on expense-free tours of Europe, provide free medical care, and make the life of congressmen more enjoyable in a number of other respects. Administrative agencies do this and for the most part questions are not raised. When private groups attempt similar activity, charges of "bribery" or worse are likely to be leveled.

Congress has attempted to deal with the public relations activities of the administrative branch by legally prohibiting the expenditure of public funds for "publicity" or the hiring of "publicity experts," unless expressly authorized.[19] Congress condones some administrative publicity that is required to carry out vital programs. It does not, however, sanction the general use of public relations men by the bureaucracy, and from time to time particular congressmen unleash attacks upon administrative agencies that have used propaganda to support programs they oppose. Officials may be called before congressional committees to answer charges that they have used illegal public relations techniques, or the matter may be referred to the Justice Department for "proper" action. However, rarely, if ever, are severe steps taken to curb propaganda by the bureaucracy, because there is no focal point of political power in the American system capable of taking such action and making it stick. For example, on occasion the President instructs agencies to support his programs in Congress, but this leads to congressional charges of "muzzling" and encouragement of administrative independence. If Congress, through individual members, charges officials with engaging in questionable propaganda in favor of important presidential programs, it means that the agencies involved receive support from the President and, with regard to legal charges, from the Justice Department.

An interesting illustration of administrative lobbying occurred in 1962, when Sargent Shriver, director of the Peace Corps and brother-in-law of President Kennedy, sent letters on official government stationery to all members of Congress in an effort to bolster the agency's request for a substantial increase in appropriations. While this was only a mild form of lobbying, Representative Lipscomb, a Republican from California, charged that public funds were being used to influence Congress, and that this constituted a legal violation. In 1948 Congress passed a bill which said in part:

No part of the money appropriated by any enactment of Congress shall, in the absence of express authorization by Congress, be used directly or indirectly to pay for any personal service, advertisement, telegram, telephone, letter, printed or written matter, or other device, intended or designed to influence in any manner a member of Congress, to favor or oppose, by vote or otherwise, any legislation or ap-

19. 18 U.S.C. 1913. 62 Stat. 792 (1948).

propriation by Congress, whether before or after the introduction of any bill or resolution proposing such legislation or appropriation.[20]

This statute has the usual ambiguous "escape clause" which provides that it does not bar communications between the bureaucracy and Congress through "proper official channels" concerning legislation or appropriations that administrators "deem necessary for the efficient conduct of the public business." Congressman Lipscomb, basing his decision on this statute, requested Attorney General Robert Kennedy to determine whether or not Shriver had broken the law. The reply from the Justice Department was that the law does not apply to the heads of agencies. The reasoning given for this was that the President has the responsibility to recommend legislative proposals to Congress, which necessitates delegation to agency heads who, as subordinates to the President, have constitutional immunity from congressional action designed to restrict them in their relations with Congress.

Regardless of statutory restrictions, administrative agencies continue to lobby Congress, and will undoubtedly continue to do so in the future. Congress may prevent the hiring of "publicity experts," but this does not prevent the agencies from employing such people under the cloak of a different title. Congressional appropriations are usually not itemized specifically, and the bureaucracy has a great deal of leeway in determining how it will spend public funds. And, regardless of particular congressional outbursts against administrative propaganda and attempts to influence legislation, the bureaucratic strength in the legislative field really stems from congressional dependence upon the information and political support that the agencies possess. Congress wants the bureaucracy to play an important role in the legislative process, and indications to the contrary are sporadic and insignificant.

Although propaganda may add to the power of an agency, it is not enough by itself to push legislative programs through Congress. In 1962, for example, Secretary of Agriculture Freeman engaged in a virtual one-man publicity campaign (although of course he used his large staff as much as possible) to persuade Congress to vote in favor of the President's farm legislation. To

20. 62 Stat. 792 (1948).

accomplish this task, he visited congressional offices and even went on television in the hope of rallying public opinion. Various other political devices were used; however, the farm bill was defeated in the House after it had passed the Senate, because the powerful Farm Bureau Federation, an important clientele group of the Agriculture Department, along with other groups and individuals of less significance, opposed Freeman. This was sufficient to counterbalance loyal Democratic forces, including the President, which supported the program.

What are the implications of the extensive use of propaganda and public relations techniques by the bureaucracy? Some observers may feel this development has grave results and may lead to the destruction of the democratic process. If the agencies can engineer consent for their programs will it not be impossible to control them within the framework of our democratic system? The problem of administrative propaganda and lobbying, however, is minor compared to the broader role the bureaucracy plays in the political system. The agencies do not gain the power they have solely through propaganda or lobbying. As far as Congress is concerned, its deficiencies in such areas as information, organization, political support, and so forth, are far more responsible for its delegation of legislative power to the bureaucracy than the public relations activities of the agencies. Although some have painted a dark picture of a society controlled by "Madison Avenue" and public relations men, it is quite obvious that congressmen are far from being so gullible. It is one thing to sell toothpaste, and quite another to sell a political program. The agencies are dealing with experienced politicians in Congress, and with experts who are also politically astute in the numerous private interest groups. It takes far more than propaganda to persuade those who have definite political interests at stake. This is not to dismiss the importance of administrative propaganda and lobbying, but only to put it into proper perspective.

## Conclusion

The American constitutional system is predicated on the belief that legislation should be formulated in a democratic and representative atmosphere. With respect to the representative function, the structure and personnel of the bureaucracy conform to many basic constitutional requirements. The administrative branch is highly representative, and it may even be argued that it is more representative than Congress. In many respects the only difference between the legislature and the bureaucracy is that the former is elected. This fact, however, does not necessarily increase the representative character of Congress. This raises the very difficult question of what constitutes adequate representation? What does the term "representation" mean? Essentially, it means that those who represent groups or individuals will act in terms of their interests as the groups or individuals themselves conceive them. Direct accountability through the electoral process is one way that may aid in bringing this about, but it is not the only way. It is quite possible for an elected official to be unrepresentative. Eventually he may be thrown out at the polls for acting in such a manner. The manipulation of party nomination procedures, the existence of one-party states, public apathy, and other factors may aid in making it possible for a congressman to be unrepresentative in relation to his constituency. It is doubtful, for example, that the Negro in many Southern states, who has been disenfranchised for considerable periods of time, feels that his interests are represented by the congressman from his district or the Senators from his state. He will more likely find greater representation in the Justice Department and other administrative agencies, and in the courts, all non-elected bodies. Moreover, internal congressional procedures, such as the seniority system, detract from the representative character of Congress as a whole.

Powerful pressure groups of all kinds will frequently be better represented in the bureaucracy than in Congress. It is quite possible they will be a more important part of an administrative constituency than of a congressional constituency. Many observers have noted instances in which agencies become the "captives" of the groups they regulate. Of course there are cases in which private groups dominate congressional constituencies, but these are less common. The congressman is dealing with individual voters who are subject to the influence of a variety of groups to which they belong or with which they identify for other reasons. Moreover, congressmen have less permanency of tenure than administrators and administrative agencies, and concentrate upon policy issues less than the bureaucracy. These characteristics of Congress tend to turn the primary attention of private groups to the administrative branch to secure effective representation. These groups are likely to develop a valuable rapport over a long period of time with the agencies that regulate them, which produces a continuity of representation that is very difficult to achieve in Congress. In addition, pressure groups also find a greater knowledge and understanding of the policy viewpoints they wish to see implemented. This is particularly true when policy fields require expert knowledge in order to comprehend the nature of the problems involved.

The group representation that the framers of the Constitution were concerned about originally was that of the states. Today, because of the proliferation and importance of private pressure groups, the representation of their interests in the formulation of governmental policy is an important element in our constitutional system. The increasing nationalization of interest groups reduces the meaningfulness of state representation. Given the greater access of these groups to the bureaucracy, constitutional representation of groups today is perhaps better achieved through the administrative process than in Congress, which is a state-oriented body. The domination of key congressional committees by Southern members of Congress in both houses illustrates dominant state and sectional influence and importance in relation to many significant national pressure groups.

The constitutional system emphasizes the importance of continuity and information. Madison and Hamilton, in *The Federalist*, felt the subjects of legislation could be divided roughly into those requiring information about the local needs of constituents and those demanding a broader knowledge of the national interest. Foreign policy, for example, falls into the latter category. Today, with the tremendous expansion in the volume and complexity of legislation there is little doubt that the bureaucracy fulfills the needs for continuity and information better than Congress. The needs of groups, most of which are national in character, have replaced the needs of individual constituents and local interests in importance to the legislative process. In effect, legislative constituencies properly understood no longer conform precisely to congressional constituencies. In addition to a change in the nature of the constituents from whom information must be obtained in the modern legislative process, the subject matter of legislation itself is more complex. In these respects although administrative policy formulation is out of line with the legislative machinery of the Constitution, it conforms in spirit to the basic theory behind the constitutional system.

Finally, Madison and Hamilton noted the importance of locating responsibility for results in the legislative process in a group that actually possesses the ability to maintain contact with appropriate policy fields from the inception of legislation to its conclusion. Here too, administrative agencies are better equipped than Congress to provide continuity to policy development. Moreover, although they are not directly accountable to the people through the electoral process, they are indirectly accountable.

The fact that Congress is more prone to veto than to initiate legislation does not necessarily detract from the vital role it plays in the political system. The bureaucracy has been established by Congress to do a job that it clearly can not do by itself, and although the administrative branch has become dominant in the legislative sphere Congress still performs important governmental functions. Major legislative changes must be approved in Congress, which frustrates the wishes of administrative agencies more frequently than they would like. Congress may also focus public attention on matters of importance through its investigations, and in this way help the electorate to become better informed. And, it remains an important representative of state and local as well as individual interests. Finally, it acts to an extent as a training and testing ground for political leaders. In the 1960 fight for presidential nominations, all the important Democratic contenders with the exception of Adlai Stevenson were Senators, and on the Republican side Richard Nixon began his career as a congressman. Of course in the past it has been unusual for Presidents to come from Congress, but this may change as the political emphasis shifts from the state to the national level. Congress remains a vital cog in the American political machine regardless of the fact that it is not the primary body initiating legislation today.

# Chapter 5    The President and the Bureaucracy

THE PRESIDENT is the man who gets things done in Washington, or so the myth goes. He is Commander in Chief, and the leader in virtually every area of government. Critics abroad and at home tend to place the blame on the President for anything they think is wrong with the United States. President Eisenhower, for example, was subjected to a great deal of foreign criticism for inaction in foreign policy just as he was criticized by many at home for failure to implement effective programs in such areas as civil rights. Richard Neustadt reports a pertinent comment of President Truman before he left the White House in 1952 as he thought of Eisenhower as President: "He'll sit here . . . and he'll say, 'Do this! Do that!' *And nothing will happen.* Poor Ike—it won't be a bit like the Army. He'll find it very frustrating." [1] Even if the President has not been a General, he is bound to be frustrated at many points, and one of the principal sources of frustration is always the bureaucracy.

The purpose of this chapter is to indicate the nature of the relationship that exists between the President and the administrative branch. The discussion will involve, first, the constitutional and political position of the Presidency in the government generally, and the relationship of this position to the functions exercised by the administrative branch; second, the instruments and difficulties of presidential control; third, the implications of the relationship that exists between the agencies and the President.

1. Richard E. Neustadt, *Presidential Power* (New York: John Wiley & Sons, Inc., 1960), p. 9.

## The President, the Constitution, and the Bureaucracy

Very frequently the beginning student of government tends to lump the Presidency and the bureaucracy together under the heading of "The Executive." It should be clear that this cannot be done. Under the Constitution the President is the executive, but this does not necessarily give him the power to control the bureaucracy. Lack of such control is often the case even when Congress makes specific provision for presidential supervision. When Congress removes all or part of an agency's operations from presidential jurisdiction, as it has done with over one hundred agencies, the President's influence is weakened even further.

In a discussion with one of his top administrators, Franklin D. Roosevelt is reported to have said:

. . . When I woke up this morning, the first thing I saw was a head-line in the New York Times to the effect that our Navy was going to spend two billion dollars on a shipbuilding program. Here I am, the Commander in Chief of the Navy having to read about that for the first time in the press. Do you know what I said to that?

No, Mr. President.

I said: 'Jesus *Chr*-rist!'

Roosevelt reportedly continued:

The Treasury . . . is so large and far-flung and ingrained in its prac-tices that I find it is almost impossible to get the action and results I want—even with Henry [Morgenthau] there. But the Treasury is not to be compared with the State Department. You should go through the experience of trying to get any changes in the thinking, policy, and action of the career diplomats and then you'd know what a real problem was. But the Treasury and the State Department put together are nothing as compared with the Na-a-vy.[2]

Variations on this story have been repeated in the administration of every President since Washington, both weak and strong, and in periods of crisis as well as of calm.

The constitutional powers the President possesses are not suf-

2. Marriner S. Eccles, *Beckoning Frontiers*, ed. by Sidney Hyman (New York: Alfred A. Knopf, 1951), p. 336.

ficient to control the bureaucracy. Constitutional ambiguity has produced congressional interference in the affairs of administrative agencies at numerous points. Even in areas in which there is a relatively clear constitutional mandate for presidential control—as Commander in Chief of the armed forces, for example—there is no automatic guarantee of presidential domination.

The constitutional system has fragmented the bureaucracy and made it virtually impossible for any one person or group to exercise meaningful control on a continuous basis. Article II of the Constitution may seem to provide for strong presidential control over the administrative branch, but the separation of powers system generally negates much of this control. Regardless of the intentions of the framers of the Constitution, the government they created did not enable the President to exercise controlling power over the bureaucracy.

On the other hand, the nature and evolution of the Presidency supports the notion that the President has important responsibilities which necessitate a high degree of presidential domination over the activities of administrative agencies. Several factors concerning the basis and evolution of the office should be emphasized in this respect. First, the Constitution, regardless of the separation of powers, makes the Presidency the focal point of leadership in our political system. This is particularly true in foreign affairs, for the framers recognized that effective diplomacy had to be conducted with dispatch from an office which possessed the ability to act with unity. But unity in the executive, as Hamilton pointed out in *Federalist 70*, is desirable for all governmental actions even though it may be of unusual importance in foreign affairs. Clearly, if such unity is to be achieved, it is necessary to make the bureaucracy accountable to the President for many aspects of its operation, and this was recommended in *Federalist 72*.

In the second place, the Constitution gives the President important responsibilities toward legislation that have become more important with the growth of the institution of the Presidency and the wane of Congress as an effective legislative body. One could argue that the legislative activities of the administrative branch should be conducted under presidential direction; that is if leadership is to be provided in the governmental system as a whole it must come from the President. Such leadership is of obvious importance in the formulation of public policy that affects not only the nation but the world.

Finally, perhaps the most important consideration of those supporting presidential control of the bureaucracy is that the Presidency today is the focal point of democracy in America. It is, in fact, the most democratic of all institutions in the world. Although the electoral college method of choosing the President still bestows an influence that is disproportionately in favor of the more populous states, the President is nevertheless the only government official elected by the people as a whole. Given the many problems Congress faces in attempting to maintain a representative character, the President is more directly connected with the electorate than Congress. Thus it may be argued that the Presidency has the greatest potentiality in our political system for the development of a combination of responsibility and accountability, which was called for by Madison, Hamilton and others with respect to the legislature. If there is a need for "decision, activity, secrecy, and dispatch" in government, to use the words of Hamilton in *Federalist 70*, combined with a dependence upon the people, the Presidency can provide it in many fields. Thus both constitutional theory and political development support the idea of presidential control of the bureaucracy, although they have worked in practice to produce a high degree of administrative independence. It should be recalled that constitutional theory, interpreted in a different light, also suggests bureaucratic independence.

## Problems of Presidential Control

Constitutional, legal, and political factors shape the kind of power the President possesses over particular administrative agencies. The President stands at the center of an extraordinarily complex and diverse system of government, and he, as all politicians and agencies, must strive to maintain a balance of political support in his favor. The numerous checks that each branch of the government has with respect to coordinate branches means that the President cannot simply order something to be done and expect it to happen. The President's order may be heeded, but not until the individual to whom the order has been given feels it is in his interest to obey: this is, of course, the essence of real authority in contrast to constitutional and legal authority. Nevertheless, it is because the Constitution fragmented the political system in the first place that the President is in such straits. Authority is never given to the President without some constitutional check in another branch of the government. And more general constitutional provisions, such as the Tenth Amendment which supports federalism, make it impossible for the President to develop a cohesive political majority.

In the discussion of Congress and the bureaucracy in the last chapter it was noted that several factors are involved in determining the power of a governmental branch or agency to legislate: (1) constitutional and legal authority; (2) political support; (3) organizational cohesiveness or unity; (4) information. On balance the bureaucracy's superiority in these areas gives it an advantage over Congress in the legislative process. The very same factors relate to the ability of the President to control the bureaucracy not only in the legislative process but with regard to all administrative functions. The ability to control, as opposed to the ability to formulate and implement legislation, also goes somewhat beyond these considerations and involves such powers as appointing and removing those over whom control is to be exercised. But the ability to appoint or remove administrative officials depends to a very large extent upon political support regardless of where the legal authority to take such action resides. Thus, in terms of the above categories, although the appointive and removal power falls initially under constitutional and legal authority, it involves political support to an equal degree. An assessment of presidential power over the administrative branch can be made by analyzing each of these categories in turn. The fact that they are interrelated should always be kept in mind.

## CONSTITUTIONAL AND LEGAL AUTHORITY

Administrative agencies are created and structured by Congress. There is no important permanent agency now existing that has not been established by statutory authority. On the other hand, during periods of national emergency, Congress may grant the President extraordinary authority to conduct the affairs of the nation, and for this purpose it may authorize him to assume complete control over the bureaucracy. Such legal authorization does not mean the President becomes a dictator, but it means that more than at any other time his principal limitation will have to come from stubborn administrators. During war, the Supreme Court and Congress retreat from the field of battle for which the Constitution so carefully provided, and the democratic process survives in the ever-present ordered conflict among administrative agencies.

World War II provides an important illustration of virtually total legal domination by the President over the administrative branch. It is instructive to observe the way in which Congress transferred to the President the legal authority to shape and control the bureaucracy during this brief period. In 1941 the First War Powers Act was passed which provided in part:

That for the national security and defense, for the successful prosecution of the war, for the support and maintenance of the Army and Navy, for the better utilization of resources and industries, and for the more effective exercise and more efficient administration by the President of his powers as Commander in Chief of the Army and Navy, the President is hereby authorized to make such redistribution of functions among executive agencies as he may deem necessary, including any functions, duties, and powers hitherto by law conferred upon any executive department, commission, bureau, agency, governmental corporation, office, or officer, in such manner as his judgment shall deem best fitted to carry out the purposes of this title [Act], and to this end is authorized to make such regulations and to issue such orders as he may deem necessary. . . . *Provided* . . . That the authority by this title granted shall be exercised only in matters relating to the conduct of the present war. . . .[3]

The Act further provided that Congress was to retain control over appropriations to the administrative branch, and that at the end of the war presidential reorganizations and redistributions of functions were to be null and void. It was on the basis of this statute that President Roosevelt established the Office of War Mobilization (OWM), a "super-agency" with virtually unlimited *authority* and, under the direction of James F. Byrnes, an un-

3. 55 Stat. 838 (1941).

usually powerful agency within carefully drawn limits.

Conflict among administrative agencies was so intense during World War II that at times the bureaucratic strife was referred to as the "battle of Washington." OWM had to contend with intrenched bureaucratic interests, and it was principally through skillful political maneuvering that it was able to achieve relative success in its attempt to coordinate the war effort. The nature of its authority was relevant primarily because Byrnes, as its chief, was considered to be an Assistant President. As Herman Somers has pointed out in his excellent account of OWM, "the ability of an over-all policy agency to implement the powers granted it, either by Congress or an executive order, depends chiefly on the status it wins within the government. The conditions of the President's order gave OWM a more elevated position than it would have enjoyed under the proposed legislation." [4] OWM was not an operating agency, but was engaged entirely in policy formulation and coordination. Lacking clientele groups, it had to rely mostly upon the President for political support. During a war period this type of arrangement may work fairly well, but even in such critical times old-line administrative agencies are unwilling to give up what they think are their prerogatives.

The experience of OWM vividly illustrates that a policy coordinating agency with all the legal authority of the President behind it, without significant congressional opposition, and with no judicial interference, cannot necessarily exercise effective control over the bureaucracy as a whole. Somers notes that "there is no doubt that Byrnes' steadfast devotion to the principles that OWM must not administer anything, must not interfere with normal operations of existing agencies, and must protect their prestige and status, was a pillar of strength for the new agency." [5] Byrnes was careful not to step beyond the bounds of his real power, regardless of his sweeping legal authority. Those who feel that the President should be "Chief Administrator" in fact should not forget the experience of OWM, nor the more general problems Roosevelt faced as he tried to exert his constitutional prerogatives

4. Herman M. Somers, *Presidential Agency* (Cambridge: Harvard University Press, 1950), p. 50.

5. *Ibid.*, p. 60.

as Commander in Chief and Chief Executive during a war period, when presidential authority is greater than at any other time.

Although the President may be given virtually unlimited legal authority over the administrative branch during wartime, in normal periods his authority is curtailed. In this respect he cannot invoke constitutional prerogatives with any degree of forcefulness or urgency. Of course the Constitution says he shall be vested with "executive power," and "may require the opinion in writing, of the principal officer in each of the executive departments, upon any subject relating to the duties of their respective offices." He is also to "take care that the laws be faithfully executed," and he is Commander in Chief of the armed forces. But these powers are mere words unless the President can persuade the bureaucracy to act in accordance with his point of view. If he cannot do this during wartime when he usually has acquiescence of Congress and the judiciary, how can he hope to achieve control over the sprawling administrative agencies during time of peace? Congress in particular becomes his adversary in normal times, and gives legal authority to administrative agencies that fortifies them against presidential intrusion into their affairs. As will soon be shown, Congress also becomes a basis of political support for agencies that wish to defy the President.

STATUTORY CHECKS ON PRESIDENTIAL POWER

The primary legal checks upon presidential power over the bureaucracy come from statutes, which determine basic organizational patterns. Statutes may limit the President's control over particular spheres of activity by assigning sole responsibility for action to an administrative agency or officer. In such situations the President loses directive power over important policy areas unless, once again, he can somehow persuade an agency to follow him. In this way much of the activity of the independent regulatory commissions is legally removed from presidential supervision; even members of his own Cabinet possess authority to act in various fields without consulting him. Moreover, Congress frequently gives independent authority to subordinate bureaus within executive departments. With such legal authority as a starting point, a stubborn official can defy the wishes of the President again and again. Unless the President wants to make an issue of such defiance and, as a last resort, ask the official to resign, there is little he can do. Many other considerations enter the picture, such as the political support of the President as opposed to that of the defiant agency or official, the President's relations with Congress and the status of his proposals in that body, congressional support of the agency, whether the administrator in question is covered by the merit system, and so forth. Although legal authority is not enough by itself to support administrative defiance of presidential wishes, there is no doubt that clear-cut legal authority for agency independence helps the bureaucracy to ignore presidential demands.

*The Merit System* · One of the most important legal limitations upon both the appointive and removal powers of the President is the merit system. The extension of the merit system during the twentieth century has resulted not only from congressional enactments, but also from executive orders. In fact, the greatest expansions of coverage have come from the President, who has of course congressional authorization to "blanket" the civil service, that is, bring it under the protection of the merit system. Under the terms of the Ramspeck Act of 1940 the President can extend this protection to virtually all of the federal bureaucracy. Regularized procedures have been established for the recruitment of personnel as well as strict rules for dismissal. Congress has further complicated the system through the creation of veterans' preferences, which aid that group regardless of talent, both with respect to recruitment and reductions in force. Some observers feel these laws have seriously reduced the effectiveness of the merit system and hampered the various presidential attempts that have been made to improve federal personnel administration.

There seems to be a paradox in the fact that the merit system, which has been expanded principally through the actions of various Presidents, is one of the greatest limitations upon presidential ability to control the bureaucracy. But it must be remembered that new agencies usually tend to be advocates of the President under whom they have been created. This follows from the necessity of administrative agencies to maintain a balance of political support in their favor. When they are first established it is usually imperative that they turn to the President for this purpose, for he is the most logical and available source of immediate support. It is not until later that they develop independent interests which may lead them into opposition with the President, who by then will most likely be a different person and possibly of a different party than the man who was in office when the agency was first established. It takes time to create effective liaison with clientele groups, and in some instances such groups will not be immediately identifiable to the newly formed agency. Frequently groups that are at first opposed to the agency will later become an important source of clientele support, as was the case with the railroads and the Interstate Commerce Commission. Perhaps an even more striking example is the Tennessee Valley Authority, which now has the strong support of groups that were at first not uniformly enthusiastic. During the Eisenhower period these groups rallied around the TVA to prevent presidential diminution of its sphere of activity.

In the twentieth century the greatest increment in the bureaucracy came during the New Deal, and all the new agencies of that period were rooted in the philosophy of the "Roosevelt Revolution," as Professor Mario Einaudi has termed this era.[6] Roosevelt may have had a "honeymoon" with Congress for only the first hundred days, but his honeymoon with the bureaucracy lasted for a considerably longer period. It was only natural that many of the men and women going into the federal service in the thirties were initially or became pro-Roosevelt, but at first they were generally not under the protection of the merit system. By placing these new civil servants under the merit system Roosevelt was taking the very course of action necessary to protect the New Deal and at the same time reward dedicated career public servants. Similarly, President Truman brought a considerable portion of the bureaucracy under the protection of the merit system before he faced the uncertainty of the 1948 election. Extending the merit system guarded the interests of the New Deal-Fair Deal public servants.

The Roosevelt and Truman actions suggest that a great deal

6. Mario Einaudi, *The Roosevelt Revolution* (New York: Harcourt, Brace & World, Inc., 1959).

of what might be called "merit system politics" can be exercised by the President. On the other hand, political interests opposed to the President are logical in their desire to have the bureaucracy put under the protection of civil service, for this prevents the President from improper political manipulation of the administrative branch while he is in office. His interests may best be served by extending the merit system only when he faces the possibility of being defeated at the polls. Thus timing becomes important. But it is inevitable politically that the merit system will continue to be extended as far as possible, and at the present time it covers well over ninety per cent of the bureaucracy.

The best example in recent years of the way in which the merit system limits the ability of the President over the bureaucracy is provided by the change that took place in 1952, when President Eisenhower became the first Republican in the White House in twenty years.[7] Although during the preceding administrations the views and actions of the agencies frequently had not been in accordance with the wishes of Presidents Roosevelt and Truman on numerous occasions, the bureaucracy was generally imbued with the idea that it should be active in the regulation of the economic life of the country and positive in making legislative recommendations to Congress and the President. Both Roosevelt and Truman preferred a bureaucracy that seized the initiative, even if this meant a certain amount of opposition to presidential desires from time to time, over a bureaucracy that was unresponsive and passive.

In general the criteria upon which the agencies were operating in 1952 were somewhat out of line with the Republican Party's officially stated position favoring the withdrawal of government from many areas in which it had participated actively during the Democratic period. President Eisenhower, who agreed basically with the Republican philosophy, faced the problem of attempting to initiate new policies through a bureaucracy that was hostile to much of what he wanted to do. The only way he could do this, or so he felt, was to make many personnel changes, but the merit

7. For an excellent account of the change in administration that took place in 1952 see Herman Miles Somers, "The Federal Bureaucracy and the Change of Administration," 48 *American Political Science Review* 131–151 (1954).

system presented a formidable obstacle. Another tack might have been to try to win the bureaucracy to his point of view, or at least act in a way which would not result in bureaucratic hostility. But for the most part this course of action was not taken, and the President set out to reduce the number of civil servants generally and in particular to concentrate upon discovering and firing disloyal and corrupt administrators. The atmosphere in the bureaucracy during the first years of Eisenhower's administration was one of suspicion and distrust. But very few changes were actually made among the permanent career officials and the bureaucracy was able to maintain its independence within the merit system. The fact that this system protected many policy-making officials raised questions in the minds of some, who felt the country had voted for a change and should have seen it implemented.

*Senatorial Confirmation* · The merit system is not the only legal obstacle faced by the President with respect to the appointive and removal powers. When Congress provides that administrative positions shall be filled by presidential appointments the confirmation of the Senate is usually required. And, of course, the Constitution requires senatorial confirmation of presidential appointments of ambassadors, "other public ministers and consuls," and judges of the Supreme Court. The President's Cabinet must be confirmed by the Senate, and although it is generally a formality, from time to time the Senate refuses to accept the President's choice; for example, at the end of Eisenhower's second term the Senate turned down the appointment of Lewis Strauss, an experienced but controversial public servant, to become Secretary of Commerce. He had formerly been Chairman of the Atomic Energy Commission during the Eisenhower administration. Although such incidents are relatively rare, the President is well aware of the need to satisfy the Senate in the appointive process. In addition to Cabinet appointments, the President has the initial power to make many thousands of appointments of subordinate officials: postmasters, judges, and so forth. Because Congress is jealous of its prerogatives it has required senatorial confirmation in virtually all these cases. The net result is that most high-level administrators engaged in policy making and adjudication must be confirmed by the Senate, and in controversial cases the President's wishes may be frustrated.[8]

The legal necessity of senatorial approval of appointments is not, however, as formidable a barrier to presidential control of the bureaucracy as the merit system. Appointments are never turned down unless there is strong political opposition capable of overcoming the political strength that always emanates from the Presidency. Moreover, Congress cannot legislate detailed provisions regarding a prospective presidential appointee. The initiative to make an appointment is considered to be an "executive" function under the Constitution. The only thing Congress can do is state general qualifications for administrative jobs, and leave the initiative in the hands of the President or another component of the administrative branch, such as the Civil Service Commission. Needless to say, in the appointive process the groups having the initiative control most of the decisions that are made.

*Legal Barriers* · The President also may face legal problems when he attempts to remove officials who occupy appointive positions outside the protection of the merit system. On assuming office, an incoming President must deal with previous presidential appointments of a different political persuasion. The Cabinet, of course, resigns upon the election of a new President even if he is of the same party as the incumbent. But key personnel in the regulatory agencies may choose to continue in office until their tenure, usually guaranteed by statute for a period of five to seven years, expires. If the President wishes to remove a member of one of these regulatory agencies he faces several legal barriers. First, the statute setting up the agency may specify that the administrator may not be removed during his term except for "inefficiency, neglect of duty, or malfeasance in office." This kind of provision implies that removal cannot be made for political reasons, which are usually the very factors behind presidential attempts to remove policy-making officials. If there is no statement of congressional policy regarding limitations upon the President's removal power over agency officials the courts may, upon a presidential attempt

8. In addition to the Strauss case a further interesting example of Senatorial refusal to accept a presidential appointment may be found in Joseph P. Harris, "The Senatorial Rejection of Leland Olds," 35 *American Political Science Review* 674–693 (1951).

at removal, step in to protect an official, provided he has been given *judicial* responsibilities by Congress. In such a case the courts may hold that regardless of the absence of a clear congressional mandate protecting a particular agency in which administrators are engaged in adjudication, there is a congressional presumption that adjudicative functions should be exercised in an independent atmosphere. This presumption may prevent presidential removal of adjudicative officials for political reasons.

These general considerations become clear upon examination of several key court cases. In 1926 the Supreme Court decided, in the historic case of *Myers v. United States,* that an 1876 law limiting the President's removal power over postmasters was unconstitutional.[9] This decision was soon to be modified. The law in question stated:

> Postmasters of the first, second and third classes shall be appointed and may be removed by the President by and with the advice and consent of the Senate and shall hold their offices for four years unless sooner removed or suspended according to law.

President Wilson appointed Myers to be a first class postmaster in Portland, Oregon, in 1917 and subsequently removed him from this position in 1920 without consulting the Senate. Myers sued for his salary in the Court of Claims, and when he received an adverse judgment an appeal was taken to the Supreme Court. Chief Justice Taft, a former President, strongly asserted in the *Myers* case the constitutional right of the President to appoint and remove subordinate officials for political and other reasons, regardless of the functions they perform. He felt such power to be implied in the constitutional provision giving the President the responsibility to see that the laws are faithfully executed, as well as in the other general executive powers stated in Article II. The main point of his argument was that the President simply cannot carry out his constitutional responsibilities if Congress interferes with his ability to control the executive branch of the government. The *Myers* opinion, which was almost belligerent in tone, as if Taft were still speaking from the White House, clearly overlooked the fact that parts of the bureaucracy, particularly the independent regulatory commissions, were purposely placed outside of

9. 272 U.S. 52 (1926).

presidential control to avoid partisan influence. Indeed, if Taft's views had been the accepted constitutional doctrine, the recent development of the bureaucracy might have been quite different, characterized by a much greater degree of administrative unity and presidential control.

The issue of the President's removal power over members of the independent regulatory commissions was raised during the New Deal and decided in 1935 by the Supreme Court in *Humphrey's Executor (Rathbun) v. United States.*[10] Humphrey was nominated to become a member of the Federal Trade Commission by President Hoover in 1931, and he was confirmed by the Senate. Federal Trade Commissioners are appointed for a term of seven years, established by Congress in the Federal Trade Commission Act of 1914. The Act states that Commissioners may be removed by the President "for inefficiency, neglect of duty, or malfeasance in office." In July, 1933, President Roosevelt requested Humphrey's resignation in a letter, giving as his reason "that the aims and purposes of the Administration with respect to the work of the commission can be carried out most effectively with personnel of my own selection." Humphrey was undecided, and another letter followed from the President in which he stated: "You will, I know, realize that I do not feel that your mind and my mind go along together on either the policies or the administering of the Federal Trade Commission, and, frankly, I think it is best for the people of this country that I should have a full confidence." Humphrey continued his refusal to resign, and in October of 1933 Roosevelt finally notified him that he had been removed. But Humphrey never agreed to his removal, and after his death in 1934 his executor, Rathbun, sued for salary he felt had been due Humphrey but never paid. The suit was brought in the Court of Claims, which certified two questions, one of a statutory and the other of a constitutional nature, to the Supreme Court to be answered before judgment could be rendered.

The questions posed for the Court in the *Humphrey* case were, first, whether or not the Federal Trade Commission Act limited the President's power to remove Commissioners except for the causes stated; second, if such a limitation existed was it in accordance with the Constitution? President Roosevelt had clearly

10.  295 U.S. 602 (1935).

indicated that the removal was for political reasons; that is, he and Humphrey did not agree on the policies the Commission should adopt. Justice Sutherland wrote the opinion of the Court, which stated that it was clearly the intent of Congress to limit the removal power of the President, and that, in answer to the second question, such a limitation was entirely constitutional. With reference to the first point the Court noted:

> The [Federal Trade] Commission is to be non-partisan; and it must, from the very nature of its duties, act with entire impartiality. It is charged with the enforcement of no policy except the policy of the law. Its duties are neither political nor executive, but predominantly quasi-judicial and quasi-legislative. Like the Interstate Commerce Commission, its members are called upon to exercise the trained judgment of a body of experts "appointed by law and informed by experience." . . .[11]

The term "impartiality" coupled with the term "non-partisan" meant policies would not be administered, that is, formulated and implemented, in terms of the interests of only one of the major parties. For this reason the President's power of removal of members of the regulatory commissions was limited, and other restraints were placed upon his ability to control the activities of these agencies. Thus the Court's conclusion correctly mirrored congressional intent to limit the President; the argument was based upon very narrow definitions which did not imply the fact that the agencies are supposed to be "political" even though not completely under the control of the President. The agencies were created as arms of Congress; they always have been as deeply involved in politics as any group in government.

After determining the intent of Congress to limit the President's removal power, the Court faced the more important question of the constitutionality of such a statutory restraint. By upholding the constitutionality of this limitation in the Federal Trade Commission Act the *Humphrey* case modified the *Myers* opinion in a substantial way. The Court noted in the *Humphrey* decision that a distinction should be made between "executive" and "administrative" functions within the bureaucracy. "Executive" functions include no responsibilities of a judicial or legislative nature; those

11. *Ibid.*, p. 624.

responsibilities are considered "administrative." Under the Constitution the President controls the executive branch, which means those agencies that perform essentially executive functions. The President may control "administrative" functions only if Congress chooses to give him the power. The Court concluded that with regard to administrators engaged in legislative and judicial functions "we think it plain under the Constitution that illimitable power of removal is not possessed by the President. . . ." [12] Moreover:

> . . . The authority of Congress, in creating quasi-legislative or quasi-judicial agencies, to require them to act in discharge of their duties independently of executive control cannot well be doubted; and that authority includes, as an appropriate incident, power to fix the period during which they shall continue in office, and to forbid their removal except for cause in the meantime. For it is evident that one who holds his office only during the pleasure of another cannot be depended upon to maintain an attitude of independence against the latter's will. [13]

Where executive functions can be identified Congress cannot limit presidential control, for the President's authority stems from the Constitution. Thus the vigorous opinion of Chief Justice Taft in the *Myers* case, which so clearly was designed to give the President virtually unlimited authority to control the entire bureaucracy, was restricted in the *Humphrey* decision to include only purely executive officials.

Although the *Humphrey* case clearly limited the removal power of the President it did not answer the question of the extent of this power when there is no statutory limitation. Causes for removal are specified for Federal Trade Commissioners, but many regulatory statutes say nothing. In such instances is the President's removal power unlimited? In 1958, in *Wiener v. United States*, the Supreme Court held that if officials are engaged in adjudicative functions the President may not remove them for political reasons. [14] Wiener had been appointed to the War Claims Commission, an adjudicative body, by President Truman in 1950, and Senate confirmation followed. The Commission was composed of

12. *Ibid.*, p. 629.
13. *Ibid.*
14. 357 U.S. 349 (1958).

three members and was to continue in existence not later than three years after the statutory limit for the filing of war claims. When President Eisenhower assumed office he requested Wiener's resignation and, when he did not receive it, removed him with the statement that: "I regard it as in the national interest to complete the administration of the War Claims Act of 1948, as amended, with personnel of my own selection." That was similar to what President Roosevelt told Humphrey upon removing him from the Federal Trade Commission. In both instances the removals were for political purposes. Noting that the War Claims Commission is clearly an adjudicative body Justice Frankfurter concluded for a unanimous Court in the *Wiener* case:

. . . Judging the matter in all the nakedness in which it is presented, namely, the claim that the President could remove a member of an adjudicatory body like the War Claims Commission merely because he wanted his own appointees on such a Commission, we are compelled to conclude that no such power is given to the President directly by the Constitution, and none is impliedly conferred upon him by statute simply because Congress said nothing about it. The philosophy of *Humphrey's Executor*, in its explicit language as well as its implications, precludes such a claim.[15]

Thus in this type of case the judiciary may limit the legal and constitutional authority of the President over the bureaucracy in the absence of statutory restraints.

## POLITICAL SUPPORT AND ORGANIZATIONAL PATTERNS

The fact that the bureaucracy is not necessarily under the control of the President, by the terms of the Constitution, nor within his jurisdiction by statute, means that the President must deal with administrative agencies in the same way he deals with other interest groups and with Congress. He must persuade the bureaucracy to go along with him, for he cannot command it to obey him. The bureaucracy, however, is not itself unitary but is composed of a multitude of agencies that very often find themselves in sharp conflict with each other. If the President were dealing with a monolithic entity in the bureaucracy he as well as other governmental and private groups might easily be dominated. But

15. *Ibid.*, p. 356.

each agency differs in terms of its authority, political support, organizational cohesiveness, and area of jurisdiction. Some agencies are of course very powerful and may be able to have their own way much of the time in their dealings with Congress, the President, and even the judiciary. But other agencies are weak in terms of the above factors relative to the strength of the President, and therefore presidential domination over their activities may follow without impediment. In such cases the agencies may turn to the President as the primary source of their own political support.

The President gains political support from a number of governmental and private groups, and from the public as a whole. If an administrative agency wishes to challenge a presidential decision ordering it to implement a particular program, it may have great difficulty unless it has strong support in Congress and from its clientele groups. The Presidency by its very nature is automatically a political force of considerable magnitude. The attention of the nation is perpetually focused upon the White House, and the President's every utterance is repeated in the various news media. He can mold public opinion, which in turn can gain him important political backing in Congress. He can also marshal the support of private pressure groups which may or may not fall outside the sphere of clientele interests of particular agencies. The fact that the President is the only nationally elected official is something no agency will overlook as it undertakes its own difficult mission of acquiring a favorable balance of political support.

Unlike Congress, and unlike many administrative agencies, the President can act with unity and with speed. Although the Presidency is now institutional, composed of a variety of staff agencies, one man still has the final power to make decisions. The political support that is gained by the Presidency can be funneled and pinpointed by one man. This kind of organizational unity is a striking contrast to the fragmented nature of Congress. An agency may divide and conquer Congress by playing off one committee against another, and by utilizing generally those congressional interests in favor of its point of view in combination with outside support to defeat those groups and individuals in Congress that may oppose it. But an agency cannot divide the Presidency if the President has firmly decided upon a particular course of action. If he has not made up his mind, the agency may be able to pressure subordinate presidential staff groups to support it and thus indirectly influence the President's final decision. But this assumes presidential indecision, which is an entirely different situation.

Although the Presidency itself may be unified to a greater extent than any other branch of the government, the President is frequently a victim of the fragmentation of the American political system. Because the Constitution requires the agreement of two houses of Congress and the President before anything can be done, the President who wishes to exercise *positive* control over the bureaucracy must have a very broad base of political support. The bureaucracy, on the other hand, will usually wish to stand pat, and hence it will primarily desire to exercise *negative* power in relation to presidential proposals. To fail to act is always easier than to act positively; that is, it is less difficult to maintain the *status quo* than to change it. The agency, then, that wishes to defy the President will actually need less political support to achieve this goal than the President will need to bring the agency into his sphere of influence. Presidential power usually requires a chain of political support which always has some vulnerable links, and a defiant agency may be particularly adept at finding these weak points.

The principal political problem the President has with respect to the agencies stems for the most part from the difficulties he faces in securing political support in Congress. Constitutional factors place the President and Congress into positions antagonistic to each other, making it impossible for the President to achieve consistent majorty support in Congress. The President may be the head of his political party, but he is far from controlling it. In fact, some of the sharpest opposition to his proposals more frequently than not will come from members of his own party in Congress. President Eisenhower, for example, often received more support for his programs from the Democrats than from the Republicans. Without the cooperation of Congress it is extremely difficult if not impossible for the President to dominate the bureaucracy, since Congress has the constitutional authority to control some of the most important aspects of administrative operation. Thus, although the President may act with dispatch and firmness in reaching decisions, his endeavors to control the agencies will fail unless Congress accedes to his wishes. But if the bureaucracy is able to dominate Congress in a particular area, it is very likely that for this very reason it will also be able to defy the President within that area.

The importance of the relationship of the President and Congress to presidential ability to control the bureaucracy may be seen in the field of administrative reorganization. The determination of legal lines of accountability generally involves the relative political support that the President, congressional groups, and the agencies are able to achieve and maintain. Moreover, reorganization is one of the few areas in which the President is likely to have a program he wishes to see implemented in relation to the bureaucracy.

Since 1949 Congress has authorized the President to reorganize the bureaucracy at his own initiative provided that within sixty days after he submits a reorganization plan to Congress neither the House of Representatives nor the Senate vetoes it by a constitutional (1949 Act) or by a simple majority (1961 Act). The first Reorganization Act, in 1939, required a veto by simple majority in both houses of Congress before a presidential plan could be rejected. This technique has not been used in the last decade although it has been desired by some, including President Kennedy, because it gives the White House more power.

Although the President has possessed the initiative to reorganize for a long time, it has not been a particularly successful presidential device in the control of the bureaucracy, even though Congress must take positive action in order to reject a reorganization plan. Many attempts have been made by the President to restructure administrative agencies, and in many important instances they have failed. A notable exception since World War II has been the creation of the Department of Health, Education, and Welfare in 1953, after several rather bitter struggles among the agencies involved.

Congressional opposition has prevented the President from reorganizing the bureaucracy to bring about better control and coordination from the White House. Presidential reorganization attempts that have failed have in addition set precedents that tend to lessen subsequent presidential enthusiasm for administrative changes. Several examples will serve to illustrate this point. There have been proposals to reorganize the independent regulatory commissions since the thirties—among them being the recommendations of the President's Committee on Administrative Management in 1937 and of the Hoover Commission in 1949. The philosophy of these reports strongly supported the idea of presidential supremacy over the bureaucracy. President Truman, acting on the basis of the 1949 Hoover Commission report, recommended various changes in the regulatory agencies which would give the President greater supervisory powers. With very few exceptions these recommendations were rejected by Congress, particularly with respect to those agencies, such as the Interstate Commerce Commission, which have powerful political support. President Kennedy again proposed similar changes to increase presidential power over the agencies, and again most of his recommendations were rejected although he managed to increase the power of the chairmen of some agencies, such as the Civil Aeronautics Board and the Federal Trade Commission; this is a step in the direction of presidential control in these and other agencies for which the President selects the chairman. The selection of the chairmen of the independent commissions and the determination of the power they should have over their own agencies have been points of contention among the President, Congress, and the agencies themselves for a long time. The trend is clearly in the direction of giving greater control to the President through this device, but he has never been able to marshal enough political support to achieve such power across the board.

Presidential problems with Congress regarding administrative reorganization involve not only the independent commissions, but all agencies that have managed to develop significant political support within and without Congress. In the past, Reorganization Acts giving the President initiative have even gone so far as to exempt the more powerful agencies. After World War II, the Reorganization Act of 1945 exempted not only a number of regulatory agencies (ICC, SEC, FTC) but also the Army Corps of Engineers, an agency with the power to defy the President even though it is one of those most directly within his constitutional and statutory chain of command. Other Reorganization Acts have similarly exempted a variety of agencies from presidential control, although this has not been the case since 1949.

Agencies are not generally powerful in Congress simply because they have outside support, but because they have cultivated good congressional relationships for many years. Particular congressional committees, charged with the responsibility of "administrative oversight"—that is, supervision—often jealously guard what they consider to be their prerogative to determine when, how, and if the agencies they oversee are to be changed in terms of organization or function. If the President makes suggestions, or strongly indicates that the location and function of agencies is essentially his responsibility and not that of Congress, these committees feel that their territory has been invaded and respond accordingly. In other respects also they may seek to protect *their* agencies from presidential interference, regardless of whether they are independent by statute or within an executive department.

Early in his administration President Kennedy became aware of the fact that the President is not necessarily "Chief Administrator." By the middle of 1962 fully 50 per cent of his reorganization plans had been turned down by Congress, including his attempt to create a new Department of Urban Affairs and Housing. His efforts to bring the regulatory agencies under closer presidential supervision were not only defeated for the most part, but elicited vigorous congressional attacks. Senator Warren Magnuson (Democrat, Washington) made it quite clear that he felt the Interstate and Foreign Commerce Committee, of which he was chairman, should have primary jurisdiction along with its counterpart in the House over all matters pertaining to the independent commissions. Other congressmen stated that President Kennedy was attempting to exercise undue influence upon these "arms of Congress." And the agencies themselves used such congressional support to oppose presidential control. Outside of the regulatory realm, not only was the establishment of a Department of Urban Affairs and Housing rejected, but Secretary Robert McNamara's centralization of activity in the Defense Department came under strong congressional attack. By the end of 1962 key congressmen were threatening to enact statutory restraints upon further centralization in the Pentagon, while at the same time bolstering the role of the individual services.

The most important conclusion that can be drawn from these considerations regarding political support and organizational patterns is that the President is the victim of the fragmentation of the political process. His inability to develop and maintain a cohesive majority detracts very substantially from his power to control the administrative branch. Each agency is free to develop whatever political support it can, and the President can do nothing to alter this situation. Where an agency depends on the President as the principal source of political support he becomes dominant; and of course a number of agencies, such as the Bureau of Reclamation or the Bureau of the Budget, fall into this category.

Congress, the judiciary, and the bureaucracy are the governmental groups that restrain the President. In addition, the existence of powerful private groups, particularly those with economic power, place restrictions upon the President. It should be added that to a considerable extent the ability of governmental (congressional committees, courts) and private groups (corporations, labor unions, farm groups, and so forth) outside the bureaucracy to resist and restrain the President is eventually manifested in the administrative branch. Particular agencies draw their strength from these groups, which in turn focus their attention upon the bureaucracy because outside of the President that is where the kind of legislative and judicial power that most directly affects their interests resides. This is true with regard to Congress as well as private groups. Thus the bureaucracy becomes a funnel into which political support is channeled from numerous sources, and for this reason it becomes in many instances the most powerful single limitation upon the President. As a whole the administrative branch represents a combination of extraordinary power. Administrative agencies never exist in a vacuum. Thus by themselves they could not challenge the President; but when Congress, private groups, and even the courts back them up there may be virtually no limit the President can place upon them. Of course the President may use the agencies as a lever against Congress, but the opposite is more often the case. When the President turns to the agencies for political support this is not indicative of his power over them, but rather of their power over him. Thus agencies may use the President as a source of support to challenge Congress, or they may use Congress in a similar way to defy the

President. In either case they are often likely to dominate the political process.

## INFORMATION AND EXPERT KNOWLEDGE

A final factor that remains to be discussed in the relationship that exists between the President and the bureaucracy is information and expert knowledge. Here, perhaps, is the most important clue to an understanding of the difficulties involved in presidential control, and the resulting administrative independence.

There is little doubt that one of the greatest limitations faced by the President with respect to the bureaucracy is that neither he nor his staff agencies are able to cope with the scope and complexity of the information that administrative agencies develop and use on a day-to-day basis in program planning and implementation. Moreover, a question should be raised as to whether it is really the responsibility of the President to acquire detailed knowledge of the myriad activities engaged in by administrative agencies.

For many years students of the Presidency and public administration have insisted upon the necessity of an expansion of the Executive Office of the President—that is, his staff agencies—to funnel information to him about the numerous areas in which he bears responsibilities. There are serious limitations in the expansion of this Office on a permanent basis, for it might result in the President becoming a captive of his own staff agencies, if he is not already a captive of the permanent operating agencies. There is nothing magical about "staff," and the concept cannot provide a cure for all the ills that befall a frequently beleaguered President.

*The Executive Office of the President* · The Executive Office of the President was first created in 1939 by executive order, and it was then composed of six agencies including the Bureau of the Budget and the White House Office, the former being transferred from the Treasury Department under the authority of the 1939 Reorganization Act. The recommendations of the President's Committee on Administrative Management and their acceptance by Franklin D. Roosevelt provided the impetus for the establishment of the Office, and it was heralded as one of the greatest achievements of the century by many both within and outside the field of public administration. At the present time in addition to the two agencies noted above, the Executive Office contains the National Security Council, established in 1947; the Council of Economic Advisers, created by the Employment Act of 1946; and the Office of Emergency Planning. These agencies represent both the *institutional* and personal part of the Presidency. Most administrators in the Executive Office have tenure under the merit system and, to a lesser extent, through general presidential practice. However, because these agencies are not operating, but staff groups, they depend for the most part upon the President for political support. About the only "clientele groups" they ever have are other agencies, which may seek to use components within the Executive Office to channel their point of view to the President. When the President is undecided, his staff agencies will more likely than not become advocates of their particular viewpoints which quite naturally produces conflict within the President's "family." Such conflict may help him to make up his own mind. Although at times the permanent operating agencies will seek to develop close contacts with the Executive Office for their own purposes, it is probably more often the case that they will consider presidential staff groups within the enemy camp and seek to short-circuit their authority. Thus, the Executive Office follows the President because its political survival depends upon him.

The Executive Office of the President is quite small, yet the agencies comprising it are supposed to collect information, plan programs, and generally assist the President, in a manner similar to congressional staff aids. Although there is greater unity within the Executive Office compared to its congressional counterpart, both face similar problems in their attempts to cope with the bureaucracy. Their primary source of information continues to be the operating agencies, and insofar as they depend upon the agencies, they must base their decisions upon the facts, and probably the opinions, supplied by the agencies. The Executive Office might be made more effective by increasing its size, but this would impair the President's control of his own staff. The Executive Office now numbers close to 1500 people, the majority of whom are employed by the Bureau of the Budget and the White

House Office. Congress uses about an equal number of persons in a staff capacity.

The problem of size of the Executive Office is not nearly as important as the issue of its proper role in relation to the agencies and to the political system as a whole. It is not size that makes a body expert, and capable of developing relevant information for use in policy formulation. The Executive Office by its very nature cannot possibly provide the President personally with enough information to enable him to supervise the legislative and other activities of the agencies. The scope and technical complexity of administrative legislation and adjudication alone precludes this, even if there were no legal and political obstacles to presidential control. What is of greater importance is the fact that the President cannot personally comprehend these areas. But why should he become personally involved? Because when the Presidency begins to function institutionally its constitutional and political responsibilities change, and what may be entirely proper for the President himself to do, or what is done with his knowledge and understanding, may pose problems when his staff does the same thing independently. When the President speaks for himself, entirely different implications arise than when a staff agency speaks for him. Thus there are not only many reasons why the Executive Office of the President *cannot* often control the bureaucracy, but questions must be raised as to whether or not it *should* do so. Before turning to the more important considerations involved in the determination of the proper relationship between the President and the administrative branch, a few additional points will be discussed to indicate the problems both the President and his staff face in attempting to gain information about the activities of the bureaucracy.

*Information-Gathering* · The most obvious problem in the gathering of information, but one that is often overlooked, is determining the questions to be asked of the agencies by the President and his staff. Are questions to be put in general terms, or are they to request specific information? Almost as soon as President Kennedy reached the White House he requested the chairmen of the independent regulatory agencies to submit brief reports to him each month containing the salient aspects of their work. Although this assured a constant flow of information, it also gave the agencies complete discretion in choosing what they would relate to the President.

Routine inquiries from the White House can cause political storms. For example, presidential assistant Sherman Adams was asked in 1954 by his close friend Bernard Goldfine to obtain information from the Federal Trade Commission about a complaint the Commission had made against him. Adams received the information, which should have been kept confidential under FTC rules, and released it to Goldfine. This incident, and other requests for information about Goldfine's affairs made by Adams to the Securities and Exchange Commission as well as the Federal Trade Commission, were subjected to congressional scrutiny and charges of improper conduct were made, forcing Adams to resign. This illustration is indicative of the fact that requests from the President or his staff for information about judicial proceedings before administrative agencies are considered improper by Congress, the agencies themselves, and the courts. This prevents presidential inquiry into one of the most significant aspects of administrative operation.

Generally, in order to know what questions to ask administrative agencies the President and his staff must be able to develop independent knowledge in the fields in which the agencies function. This does not mean that the Executive Office and the President have to equal the expert knowledge of the agencies, but they must possess a certain degree of detailed understanding, which can be achieved in only relatively very few fields.

In areas where precise presidential policy has been developed —for example, defense—there is little doubt about the ability of the President and his staff to ask significant questions of the bureaucracy and gain responsive answers. Even here agencies are sometimes defiant, but their ability to ignore presidential wishes will depend upon legal and political factors and not upon a monopoly of the information necessary for decision making.

These considerations lead to the conclusion that the activities of the bureaucracy in relation to the President may be placed roughly into two categories: (1) those that relate to a presidential program that has been defined with some degree of precision; (2) those that fall outside the boundaries of a presidential program. The second category arises because the Presidency cannot be knowledgeable enough to formulate a "policy" to guide most of the activities of the administrative branch, nor will the President's general programs involve all of the agencies.

What degree of presidential control of the bureaucracy exists if by necessity and by choice the President is not concerned directly about a great deal of what the agencies are doing? In some instances the Bureau of the Budget may step in to *coordinate* agency policies that it feels are in conflict. But this does not work well, particularly if the agencies concerned have powerful political backing and choose to ignore "Budget" by failing to clear legislative and other proposals through it. If the operating agencies lack the power to defy "Budget," they may watch with frustration while the Bureau of the Budget tries to formulate policies, more or less on an *ad hoc* basis, with little if any consultation with the President.

There is little doubt that the Bureau scans the operations of the administrative branch rather closely, but it is equally clear that it does not control substantive policy or judicial decisions made by the agencies. This is not its purpose. Nor is it the purpose of the Executive Office as a whole. The agencies are given freedom within their spheres of activity by the President and his staff unless the interests of the White House are directly affected.

The opinions of the agencies, of course, always play an important part in the formulation of any presidential policy and in many instances this influence will be decisive. But although the agencies may have extraordinary power to shape presidential programs, both the President and his staff will become personally involved and, presumably, develop an independent understanding of the issues. Once a program has been decided upon, agency action can be judged on the basis of whether or not it has been in accordance with presidential wishes. At this point and probably only at this point does it become meaningful to talk about presidential control of the bureaucracy, for if the President has a definite program it is clearly in his interest to make certain the agencies do not attack it generally or nullify it through their actions.

Examples of areas of administrative activity which do and do not relate to presidential programs may aid in clarifying the previous discussion. First, consider a few fields in which the President usually does not have a defined policy. Most regulatory fields fall into this category. For example, the President does not have a program for air safety and the regulation of the airlines and airways generally. This he leaves to the primary agencies involved, the Civil Aeronautics Board and the Federal Aviation Agency. There is simply not enough time for either the President or his staff to master the numerous complex details that are involved in formulating a policy. Likewise, in other regulatory fields, such as communications, transportation, stock exchanges and securities regulation, public utilities, and sometimes anti-trust policy, there is usually no well-defined presidential policy. In addition to these and other regulatory fields there are numerous areas of administrative activity with which the President is necessarily unconcerned. For example, much of the day-to-day work of such Departments as Health, Education, and Welfare, Interior, Commerce, and so forth, is not related to any particular presidential policy. And information concerning the judicial activities of the agencies is generally excluded from presidential purview.

On the other hand, definite presidential policies exist in such crucial areas as defense and foreign affairs. The strength of our ground forces, the kinds of weapons we will use, where they will be located, the circumstances under which they will be employed, and so forth, are matters on which all modern Presidents have policies. In cases of national emergency the National Security Council will be called into session, chaired by the President, and although possible decisions will be discussed in such meetings the President makes the final choice. In areas such as these the President is solely responsible for what is done; thus, it is desirable that he be able to gain adequate information from the bureaucracy to formulate policies which will in turn be implemented.

The fact is that the Presidency as an institution cannot carry out its major responsibilities and at the same time control and coordinate all the activities of the administrative branch. Thus, information becomes one of the vital factors of presidential control, and its complexity produces a high degree of administrative independence that otherwise might still come from political, constitutional, and legal factors. This becomes abundantly clear when one realizes that an administrative agency may select a course

contrary to definite presidential policy. An interesting current illustration is the Federal Reserve Board, which has threatened to
carry out money policies in direct opposition to the wishes of the
Democratic administration. The Federal Reserve has done so in
the past; it has both the legal authority and the political support
to be successful, even in the face of a clear-cut presidential program.

## Conclusion: Should the President Control the Bureaucracy?

The realities of the relationship between the President and the
bureaucracy must be recognized. In terms of our Constitution and
the nature of our political system today it is not possible, necessary, or desirable that every aspect of administrative activity be
controlled by the White House. If the President were to concentrate on this task it would mean a virtual abdication of his more
important responsibilities. Delegation of authority and power is
an integral part of our government, and it must be recognized
that within broad areas administrative agencies are the primary
groups responsible for legislation and adjudication.

Critics of this position contend that if the President cannot control administrative activity it is up to his staff to step in and fill
the gap. Here it should be noted that it is the President who is
elected by the people, not his staff. Moreover, because his staff
is detached from operating activities it can in some instances function secretly and without accountability except to the President
himself. The previous chapter pointed out that the bureaucracy
is a highly representative branch of our government, in many
respects more representative than Congress; it should be added
that the bureaucracy may be more representative in some ways
than the President, and certainly more than the presidential staff.
Private groups will very likely get more knowledgeable and more
direct representation in those agencies to which they have access,
than in the Presidency. The democratic process must reflect group
demands as well as the more nebulous demands of the public at
large. The President is the best representative of the latter, but
the agencies are often the more effective representatives of the
former.

Finally, it should be noted that in our political system the President is not always motivated to control the bureaucracy—a key consideration raised before with respect to Congress. The President's political survival depends upon a nationwide electoral process in which his personality and a few key issues determine the outcome. He need not always know what policies the agencies are following, or what decisions they are making in their judicial spheres: they are the primary concerns of the agencies themselves, and their political survival may depend upon the policies and decisions they carry out.

The American Presidency is a great institution, but the President is not in fact "Chief Administrator." He cannot, nor does he wish to, control all the complex activities engaged in by the administrative branch. In many key areas of presidential responsibility he demands, and generally receives, loyalty from administrative agencies. But in other fields the agencies function with partial autonomy in the policy spheres that have been assigned to them by Congress.

# CHAPTER 6 Conclusion

A MAJOR QUESTION remains: How does American bureaucracy fit into our system of constitutional democracy? Does it conform to our pattern of limited government? Is it responsive to popular demands that arise from time to time for changes in government policies? An emphatic "yes" can be given in answer to each of these questions. American bureaucracy may not harmonize perfectly with the forms of our Constitution, but it is compatible with its spirit. It occupies a responsible position within our political system.

American bureaucracy is an independent force, and from its independence it draws much of its strength and prestige. It is a powerful and viable branch of government, not properly subject to complete control by Congress, the President, or the judiciary. But its independence does not mean that it possesses total discretion. It functions within a checks-and-balances system in much the same way as the original three branches of government. Its boundaries of action are set by Congress, and these must not exceed constitutional limits as determined by the courts. The President plays a varied role in relation to the agencies, but is unable and unwilling to supervise all of their myriad activities.

It is difficult to grasp the concept that the bureaucracy is not subordinate to one or more of the three initial branches of American government. But the fact is the three primary branches have necessarily supported the creation of a semiautonomous bureaucracy as an instrument to enable our government to meet the challenges it has faced. Given the needs of modern government for economic regulation, specialization, continuity, and speed in the dispatch of business, to mention only a few, it is the bureaucracy that has stepped in to fill the gap created by the inability of the other branches to fulfill all of these requirements. The other branches, particularly the Presidency and the Supreme Court, have also greatly expanded their ability and willingness to meet the challenges of the twentieth century, but they could not possibly solve by themselves the extraordinary problems that have confronted our government.

The fact that American government has been able to change to meet demands placed upon it while at the same time preserving constitutional democracy is not always fully appreciated. There has been much wringing of hands among some political scientists about "the deadlock of democracy," the inability of the President and Congress to work together through a disciplined party system.[1] This deadlock presumably prevents meaningful participation by the electorate. But neither parties, Congress, nor even the electoral system should be thought of as the only critical elements in our governmental system. The President can act without relying upon them in many instances, and for this very reason our country has survived where otherwise it might have foundered. And the bureaucracy, which is actually a more representative body than Congress, combines essential democratic ingredients at the same time that it formulates important policy. Administrative agencies, removed from the electoral process, can take action without consulting Congress, and such action is as responsive to the demands and needs of the community as any that Congress could take even if there were no "deadlock." In this respect American bureaucracy provides in part an answer to the stalemate that often exists between the President and Congress. But it should be remembered that the factors leading to the supremacy of the administrative branch in the formulation of governmental policy and in many areas of adjudication would produce exactly the same result if the parties were unified and if there were no executive-legislative conflict.

The one difference that would result from greater cohesion between the President and Congress would be a more unified bureaucracy under the legal authority of the President, as Congress would no longer be so motivated to make administrative agencies independent. But this would not diminish the overall role of the bureaucracy, which would maintain much of its independence through political support, control over information, continuity in office, and so forth. In this respect it would be a change more in

1. See, for example, James M. Burns, *The Deadlock of Democracy* (Englewood Cliffs: Prentice-Hall, Inc., 1963).

legal forms than in substance. But on the other hand it would destroy the balance of powers among the branches of government that has always been considered essential to the preservation of freedom in America. It would permit the government as a whole to overwhelm the community if it were bent upon a particular course of action, particularly because all of the vast powers of administrative agencies would be combined under presidential and party direction. And where no clear party policy existed, which would be a very wide area indeed, the bureaucracy would go its own way, with less interference, less committee surveillance by members of Congress used to independent thought and investigation, than is presently the case.

It is, of course, unrealistic to think that American government can in the foreseeable future develop presidential-congressional unity through our political parties. What is suggested here is that this is neither desirable nor necessary because of the dynamic and responsive nature of the bureaucracy and, in other areas, the Presidency and the courts. Moreover, an independent and individualistic Congress contributes much to our political system in spite of its various deficiencies.

With the exception of the initial executive departments, administrative agencies were created long after the Constitution was written. The precepts of constitutional democracy thus had a chance to become firmly embedded as part of the American political tradition before the administrative branch began to take shape as a significant force threatening the governmental balance of powers. This tradition has been a permanent influence shaping old and new political institutions into its own distinctive pattern, and the bureaucracy has not been an exception.

The administrative branch did not escape the effects of the separation-of-powers system, which caused a fragmentation of bureaucratic power. It did not escape the democratic forces that led to the merit system, which lessened the possibility of an elite bureaucratic class developing. Moreover, it did not escape the remnants of the spoils system, which guaranteed a circulation of the elite at the top levels. American bureaucracy is not run by a privileged group, but by men and women of diverse backgrounds. It is not separate from the community at large, but an integral part of it. Finally, the bureaucracy has always been responsive to interest groups, an important democratic characteristic of all branches of American government.

As long as the activities of administrative agencies are viewed as being political, there will be little chance of a movement developing either within or without the bureaucracy to detach it from the political system as a whole. It is because the bureaucracy possesses such important political functions that Congress, the President, the judiciary, and private-interest groups make certain that some control is exercised over it. If "administration" were thought of as something apart from the political process, this might lead to the feeling that it should be detached from the demands of the political system. But American bureaucracy is responsive to the standards of constitutional democracy because it is an integral part of the "politics" that go to make up our governmental system. It is not neutral. Its procedures and its decisions are not subject to scientific formulation by administrative experts acting alone. Administrative agencies are forced to pay attention to political demands from many points in order to survive. This fact makes an important contribution to our system of administrative responsibility.

As American government continues to grow in response to the heavy demands that will inevitably be placed upon it, it is certain that the bureaucracy will continue to occupy a position of central importance. Administrative agencies will have more discretion in the future than they now have as public-policy needs increase and become more complex. But this growth of bureaucracy is not a cause for alarm. It adds an important new dimension to our government. American bureaucracy takes its place as an equal partner with the President, Congress, and the judiciary. Its existence not only increases the ability of our government to meet the challenges of the twentieth century, but also enhances the meaning of constitutional democracy.

# Index